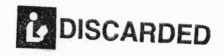

SOLDIERS AS STATESMEN

The Second Military History Symposium
Royal Military College of Canada

1975

SOLDIERS AS STATESMEN

Edited by

PETER DENNIS and ADRIAN PRESTON

CROOM HELM LONDON

First Published 1976.
© 1976 by Peter Dennis and Adrian Preston

Croom Helm Ltd, 2-10 St John's Road, London, SW11

ISBN 0-85664-300-9

Printed and bound in Great Britain
by Redwood Burn Ltd, Trowbridge and Esher

CONTENTS

Introduction. *Adrian Preston*   9

Hindenburg. *Martin Kitchen*   55

Franco. *Hugh Thomas*   79

Lord Byng in Canada. *Roger Graham*   93

Eisenhower. *Stephen Ambrose*   113

De Gaulle. *John Cairns*   135

Contributors   177

Index   179

Preface

The essays in this book are based on papers presented at a symposium held at The Royal Military College of Canada, Kingston, Ontario, in April 1975, at what it is hoped will become an annual occasion for the meeting of scholars from North America and Europe.

Without the generous financial support of the Department of National Defence and the Canada Council we could not have brought our speakers to RMC and enjoyed their stimulating presence for several days.

To our contributors and to those who came to hear these papers, and to David Croom, who encouraged us in their publication, we express our thanks.

PD
AP

Introduction

ADRIAN PRESTON

'It is much to be a great general and a great ruler of men: it is more to be also a great gentleman and a great patriot. It is more than all to exalt forever in a great nation the standard of discipline and of duty.'

Sir John Fortescue on the Duke of Wellington

I

'The Duke is a soldier — a bad education for a statesman in a free country.'[1] Thus, epigrammatically, did Sir Walter Scott sum up one of the more enduring and romantic myths of modern political history. For Scott, as for the truculent and war-weary generation for whom he spoke, needed no reminder of the monstrous excesses to which military tyranny and revolutionary infection might lead. For over twenty years, in the wars against Revolutionary and Napoleonic France, they had endured mounting deprivations on their individual liberties on a scale that made even the grim spectres of Cromwell or, perhaps more significantly, the Duke of Cumberland seem almost welcome. For Scott, as for most of the aristocracy, the exaltation to Prime Minister of the most famous soldier in Europe, who combined within his person the chief military offices of State, seemed a clear invitation to Caesarism or civil war. But however wrong-headed, immoral and repellent Scott judged it to be, and however ludicrously suspicious his reaction might seem, we live in a later generation, which has witnessed the disintegration of the dynastic empires of the Ottomans, Habsburgs, Hohenzollerns and Romanoffs, and the dissolution of the colonial empires of Britain, France and Holland. There has been a proliferation of weak and unstable 'successor' states in which military

9

government rapidly becomes an entrenched and immovable necessity, so that we accept the phenomenon of soldier-as-statesman as a problem with which all societies must eventually deal at some stage of their development, in some cases with depressing frequency.

The egregious suggestion, so congenial to Whig Romantics, that politicians and historians could ignore the incidence of war and the influence of armed forces in their calculations, has today only to be stated to be dismissed. So long as the sanction of force lies at the root of all social organisations and organised military power is an ineluctable constituent of international politics, there will always remain the possibility that soldiers will take advantage of some breakdown in orderly traditions of civic power and thrust themselves upon the State: not so much to cow rebellion at home or pursue enemies abroad, as to re-establish order and stability, retrieve the national honour lost in battle and create the right conditions for rapid and steady modernisation. The manner in which this possibility is contained will largely determine the political character and durability of the State. From the breakdown of the monarcho-feudalist and ecclesiastical authority of the late Middle Ages until the end of the eighteenth century, the really vital problem of civil-military relationships was not that generals might somehow seize supreme political power but rather that the princes within the political aristocracy might seize the armed forces of the State and turn them to their own account. Men like Cromwell or Washington, who in middle age had turned to soldiering in the cause of revolution and civil war, carved out by intuitive skill, stubbornness or sheer good luck imperishable reputations, and in the New Model and Continental Armies took the first steps towards a more orthodox professionalism which became synonymous with the new secular or revolutionary State.

But with the advent of the age of political and ideological revolution which opened in 1776, the question reversed itself. In the struggles between 'nations in arms' inaugurated by the American and French revolutionary wars, followed by the great American and German wars of national unification and reaching their climax in the two world wars which have dominated our own century, the Clausewitzian dogma of the decisive battle became central to all strategic doctrine and national policy. Among the great or nascent industrial states of the northern hemisphere, entangled as they were in a complex web of imperial rivalry and economic necessity, organised military power and the naked determination to use it became the sole determinant of national destinies. During this period, the formal influence of the profession of arms, in its clubs, colleges and institutes, in its trade journalism and official historiography, in its exclusive and austere staff system and its formidable standards of precision and thoroughness in planning and advice, became more distinct, potent and direct at every level of political society. The virtual military dictatorship of the German General Staff during the First World War, and the no less extraordinary powers enjoyed by the Anglo-American Combined Chiefs of Staff in the Second is the result of this influence. At the same time, paradoxically, war had become a matter of competing economic and human resources, scientific and administrative expertise, industrial productivity, social stability and public morale — factors in themselves as significant in the outcome as the operations of the armed forces in the field. Henceforth no State could afford to construct its defence policy or conduct its wars on the basis of strictly military appreciations of the world situation. The new interdependence of the military, economic, scientific and industrial components of national power, which was the distinguishing characteristic of the wholesale democratisation of modern war, was accompanied by the erosion of the artificial distinctions which had traditionally, and sometimes danger-ously, isolated the soldier from the State, as they had isolated the study of armed forces and military histroy from its con-stitutional, political and economic context. It was very largely to break down this unhealthy state of civil-military apartheid and the bitter interdepartmental disputes which had so tragic-ally disfigured the strategic conduct of the First World War that the United States had set up the Industrial War College in 1922 and the United Kingdom the Imperial Defence College in 1927. Before tendering their expert advice to governments and in managing their own campaigns abroad, soldiers were now compelled to take into account a wide range of variables: local politics, national finance and manpower, strategic possibilities and logistical limitations and allied and neutral intentions and susceptibilities. It was no use fretting, as the overly-fastidious

Canadian general, A.G.L. MacNaughton, was reputed to have done, that he could not keep his mind on the war if he was always having to worry about the military ramifications of the Statute of Westminster.[2] There is no better evidence of the blurring of distinctions between political decision and military action than the return into common strategic parlance of such phrases as 'military politics', 'political general', 'soldier-statesman' and 'military governor', which seemed more appropriate to the age of Marlborough.

After 1945, with the advent of the age of nuclear deterrence and insurrectionary warfare, the distinctions were diffused still further, but that did not make the problem any less complicated or pernicious. From Michael Howard's peculiarly Eurocentric point of view in 1957,[3] governments could no longer 'be suspected of using military force to crush internal opposition', nor military leaders 'of nurturing Caesarist ambitions'. The inaccuracy of that claim was manifested by subsequent events in France, Greece and Czechoslovakia, and by the recent Congressional revelations in the United States about CIA and FBI plots to assassinate their own countrymen. The economically weaker states of the West — Turkey, Greece, Spain and Portugal — and some of the stabler but increasingly embattled successor states in the Middle and Far East, such as India and Israel, are finding themselves encircled by a protracted guerilla struggle for which a pre-emptive nuclear strike may seem the only appropriate military solution. These states cannot be expected to fight their battles along the conventional lines of World War Two, and the incidence of military dictatorship and statesmanship seems to be growing rather than diminishing. Already black Africa seems to have gone the way of Latin America.

The contemporary phenomenon of soldier-as-statesman — as distinct from that of military politics, political generalship or military government — even if confined to the major powers of the West during the period embraced by the two world wars, as these studies are, raises questions of profound political, sociological and historical importance. At a certain level of analysis, the problem is largely biographical and idiosyncratic. Precisely what kind of man is it who manages to triumph over and manipulate not merely the accidents of war or revolution but the rigid conventions and deep beliefs of a profession into whose service his whole life had been previously committed? In what combination of circumstances is power seized or thrust upon him?

When we turn to soldiers as heads of military governments, the problems become more complicated and self-contradictory. For instance, what objectives do they pursue: social revolution, modernisation or the mere consolidation of military interests? How do they establish and maintain their legitimacy and prepare the way for alternative rule? How do they resolve the fundamental contradiction between the requirements of dictatorship and the appearance of democracy? To what extent and in what ways do the attributes of military professionalism — order, system, secrecy and a disdain for inconclusive debate, messy compromises and flabby decisions — sharpen or diminish his perception and practice of statecraft? Indeed, by what criteria are soldiers as statesmen to be judged at all, and if so is it proper that these criteria should be different from those usually applied to lawyers and businessmen? Is it possible in any event to deduce such a pattern of common criteria with which their behaviour and performance can be assessed or explained? Indeed, one of the most singular failings of modern American political science has been its assumption that the incidence and nature of military government throughout the Third World, which often has its roots in an indigenous theocratic militarism which has lain dormant under foreign occupation, could be satisfactorily explained in accordance with Huntington's classic but crude criteria, which were originally defined at a time when American politicians and strategists saw themselves engaged in a gigantic ideological crusade.

It may be suggested that the various manifestations of military government are now so widespread and frequent in occurrence as to have become a permanent and significant condition of international politics, and as such can no longer be conceived of in terms related only to the objectives or morality of American foreign policy. Military governments and statesmen, like the revolutionary and civil wars which usually precede them, are expressions of unique indigenous and historical forces, and there is some evidence that after Vietnam and Watergate American scholarship is beginning to accept that fact sympathetically.[4] On the other hand, no free society can afford to reject out of hand Scott's suspicions that soldiers by temperament and training are unequal to the demands of high statesmanship and may therefore be tempted to resort to more familiar but more arbitrary methods of government. And it is for this reason that the experiences of Britain, of the United States and above all of France (where the expressions *coup d'état* and man-on-horseback were originally coined) of soldiers as statesmen in the nineteenth and twentieth centuries are perhaps the most fascinating.

II

Yet for all its complexity and significance, professional historians have surprisingly ignored the question of soldiers-as-statesmen. The British, true to their national intellectual traditions, have been largely content to let biography speak for itself; but equally faithful to those traditions these biographies have been written by journalists, former civil servants and that incomparable band of amateur *littérateuses* led by Lady Longford and her daughter Antonia Fraser. It is true that since the mid-fifties American scholars have dominated the theory and sociology of military professionalism and government as a distinct field of intellectual enquiry which, like the theory of nuclear deterrence, they had virtually to create from scratch.[5]

Several factors were responsible for this obsession, which was by no means restricted to academic philosophers. In the first place, the post-war interest in the Third German Reich aroused by the Nuremberg Trials, the war memories of German generals and books like Liddell Hart's *The German Generals Talk* centred 'on the part played by the German Army in facilitating Hitler's rise to power and the degree of responsibility which it must bear in formulating and executing his policies.' How did it come about that the Wehrmacht and its leaders, which under Ludendorff in World War One had dominated national policy and even under Hitler enjoyed a considerable autonomy, could loyally sacrifice its interests, its will and its integrity to a régime it heartily despised? By what perverse combination of methods — intimidation, flattery and indoctrination — did Hitler dominate them? What was the special nature of Army-Party relationships in a totalitarian state? Secondly, the conduct of World War Two, involving as it did the construction of elaborate inter-allied and inter-departmental machinery to co-ordinate the competing requirements of domestic affairs, foreign policy and military action in the central formulation of grand strategy, seemed grounded on one gigantic contradiction which contained within itself the makings of endless historical controversy. On the one hand there were the principal War Directors — Churchill, Roosevelt, Stalin and Hitler — who as their own Ministers of War or Commanders-in-Chief were interfering directly with the grand tactical operations of their armies, summarily removing dour one-eyed generals who through lack of resources, were unable to provide the swift and spectacular victories which public moral required. On the other hand, as the official histories and military memoirs make clear, the Anglo-American Combined Chiefs of Staff, working in continuous personal contact with Prime Minister and President to the exclusion of their civilian departmental Ministers, had enjoyed a degree of power unparalleled in the history of coalition warfare. The British chiefs had won and held that power with remarkably good grace in the face of Chruchill's psychotic bullying and atrocious bad manners, but American politicians feared that if perpetuated in the post-war machinery for the military government of Germany and Japan, it might eventually become a sinister force in domestic politics. Few Americans bothered to notice in this regard that Wavell and Mountbatten had become the first and last soldier-Viceroys of the Indian Empire.

Thirdly, the conspicuous refusal of the Indian Army to exploit the communal factionalism which so tragically beset the final stages of India's road to independence had aroused false hopes that the successive waves of decolonisation which swept westward through the Middle East and black Africa would somehow result in a buffer zone of stable, democratic states whose foreign policies were aligned with, and their economies dependent upon, those of the United States. Instead, these successor states discovered with chastening speed that they were no longer inert motifs in the grand tapestry of Empire but were independent sovereign territorial entities with vulnerable and vital interests and borders to defend against potentially hostile neighbours. Unlike India, most had failed to develop the administrative and judicial institutions, skills and traditions with which the ambitions of their generals might be effectively curbed and the anxieties of their politicians temporarily allayed. In these circumstances only the armed forces constituted in themselves the collective strength, expertise, organisation and outlook necessary to defend and develop the national resources in a world that at a much higher level was dominated by the economic and ideological rivalries of continental Russia, America and China.

Finally, the decisive defeat of dismemberment of France, Germany, Italy and Japan, the emergence of organised movements of national resistance and revolution in occupied territories, the imminent disintegration of the British, French and Dutch colonial empires, and the advent of an atomic technology all thrust upon the United States an unprecedented and inescapable range of strategic responsibilities and commitments in Europe, the Middle East and Asia, which would require a powerful, costly and permanent military establishment to defend against the implacable designs of Soviet Russia and with which it was historically, intellectually and psychologically ill-equipped to deal. Between Pearl Harbor and Hiroshima, America's position as a world power had been dramatically and irrevocably transformed. The realisation of that transformation awoke feverish discussion as to how that status could be reconciled with the mythology of a community — the first of the modern revolutionary states — which had always believed itself to be not only anti-militarist but anti-imperial and downright isolationist as well.

The characteristics of that discussion should be noted. It was in the first place overwhelmingly American and tied to the requirements of American defence policy. The pioneering works of Huntington and Janowitz,[6] crude and sweeping though they were in their use of history, nevertheless provided an intellectual framework of analysis which no serious student of the problem could henceforth ignore. Yet in Britain there still exist no studies of comparable weight and originality of the officer corps of the Royal Navy and the British Army — of the structure of British military politics — although there has been a mounting interest in the Indian Army which for all intents and purposes was the closest thing to a Continental Army the British Empire possessed. But even here, as in studies of British naval administration and policy, the best work has been largely American.

Secondly, as a field of study the central problem of civil-military relations — the political control of military power for social purposes — was from the start monopolised by sociologists and political philosophers with scant regard for history. If they could not discover a uniquely American problem in studies of the American West or the Revolution, they tended to create one, and to solve it by ripping it out by the roots, where a more dispassionate study of the recent past might have sufficed. To cynical European eyes, the amount of intellectual energy so furiously expended seemed almost indecently disproportionate to the triviality, naïvety and simple-mindedness of much of the discussion. John McCoy's remark that American military government in Germany 'was the nearest thing to a Roman Proconsulship the modern world afforded'[7] betrayed an astonishing ignorance not only of the strategic factor in British imperial administration and the British use of soldiers as colonial governors but of his own country's prior experience of military government in the South after the Civil War, in Cuba and in the Philippines. Not for another twenty years would the serious study of American military history, temporarily usurped by that of nuclear strategy and civil-military relations, get into its stride, belatedly providing the sound historical underpinning which those contemporary studies had conspicuously lacked.[8] In the third place, the earliest works on civil-military relations excluded explicit consideration of the more esoteric and remote manifestations of military government, assistance and alliances, both in developing and Communist countries, which would assume greater importance as the de-Stalinisation of American perceptions of Soviet Russian policy and the process of decolonisation stepped up in pace. Yet when American scholars in the early sixties began to turn their attention to the experiences of new states in adjusting to the problems of military professionalism, power and government, they did so as a kind of academic Peace Corps, anxious to prove that military governments were prime agents of modernisation and social reform.[9] Only after military government in Africa and the Middle East had been given a decent trial — in this case ten years — was it possible to measure promise in terms of real performance and to arrive at a more candid and pragmatic view of the realities and necessities of this form of government.[10]

From all this it followed that in spite of the fact that both Eisenhower and De Gaulle were the Presidents of their respective countries, no one bothered to take the question of soldiers-as-statesmen very seriously, possibly because in neither case did it imply the breakdown of those social and political controls with which they were otherwise obsessed. The fear that American generals might obtain enough influence over foreign policy and public opinion to make their accession to political power seem necessary and desirable had been awakened as early as 1942 during the first discussions about the post-war administration of occupied Germany. While the British might off-handedly query the suitability of particular generals — Montgomery and Templer, for instance — as potential governors-in-occupation, the Americans questioned the whole principle of permitting soldiers to enjoy, for however short a period of time, a taste of supreme power. Would they not become insatiable or addicted, carry awkward ambitions back to the United States or refuse to relinquish their quite extraordinary and extra-constitutional powers? But as the balance of strategic power within the Grand Alliance shifted in America's favour in 1943, this uneasiness about the possibilities of Caesarism abroad was absorbed into the larger question, already mentioned, of the political and social implications of the maintenance of a powerful and permanent military establishment at home.[11] That Clay and MacArthur, Marshall and Eisenhower should all enjoy great political power was proof of the axiom that those who conduct war are best equipped to construct peace, and of America's determination to grasp the nettle of its new and inescapable world responsibilities. It also demonstrated the persistence of a peculiar American tradition stretching back through Roosevelt, Grant, Washington and dozens of other more obscure generals in the White House, the notion that Continental states born of revolution can never be so unmilitary as they would like to suppose.

III

What exactly do we mean by 'soldier' and what by 'statesman', and by what criteria were we led to select the subjects of the present studies? Is it length of service or degree of commitment and conformity to its ideals which principally distinguishes the regular member of the profession of arms from his paramilitary and occasional counterpart in the militia, volunteers, the National Guard or the Yeomanry? Must the soldier have won his reputation as a commander, a reformer, an administrator or a theorist? in orthodox or irregular warfare? in grand or minor campaigns? or, and this is in particular relevant to new states, need he have won a reputation at all? Is it significant that the French experience of soldiers-as-statesmen in the nineteenth and twentieth centuries can be identified with a sequence of military defeats (Napoleon after 1793, MacMahon in 1870, Pétain and De Gaulle in 1940) while in America it followed a succession of military victories (Washington after the Revolution, Jackson after the War of 1812, Grant after the Civil War, Roosevelt after the Spanish-American War and Eisenhower after the Second World War)? Is it possible to evaluate according to a common set of criteria the statesmanship of a soldier working obscurely alongside Ministers and officials within the central organisation of defence, that of the soldier governing a remote, vulnerable and strategically vital colony and that of the soldier administering an occupied war zone in which the institutions of public order and security have been destroyed or paralysed? And if we allow that not all generals, let alone ex-corporals and ex-colonels who are the most successful revolutionaries in new states, live up to Wavell's classic criteria of a Great Captain, should we insist that all 'statesmen' exercise the chief executive authority as Head of State? Do we include therefore men such as Cromwell, Washington or even Mao Tse-tung who belatedly turned to soldiering in the cause of revolution and then imposed upon that revolution their own conceptions of armed professionalism and national statehood? In eighteenth-century Britain and the nineteenth-century United States, and to a lesser extent France, Prussia and Russia in the nineteenth century, there was a golden age of military politics, political generalship and colonial military government, and in the absence of the constraints of organised military professionalism and stable political parties, men floated easily between politics and war. Do we include such men, perhaps serving in some minor campaign to project their political image and appeal and, if successful, immediately shedding all the panoply of high command to resume the common touch of the political candidate? Do we include professional soldiers who in the routine of Continental tradition become War Ministers or Ambassadors and through sheer longevity, capacity and

independence of judgement exercise a marked influence upon
the constituencies they serve? General Ignatieff, as Russian
Ambassador to Turkey from 1864 to 1874, spent ten years
secretly plotting the overthrow of the country to which he was
accredited. Do we include soldiers who served as Secretaries of
State such as Marshall, or as post-war military governors-in-
occupation such as Templer or MacArthur, or as military
attachés, whose views about the capabilities and intentions of
potentially rival military powers were, except in certain
notorious cases, decidedly less alarmist than those of the
Ministry they represented? What about colonial Governors or
Viceroys, such as Butler in South Africa, Allenby in Egypt and
Wavell in India, whose attitudes towards local nationalistic
movements were so embarrassingly progressive, straightforward and realistic as to bring about their own recall at the
hands of governments who couldn't stomach them? What are
we to make of a man like Captain Evelyn Baring (later Lord
Cromer) whose deflatory influence upon the more grandiose of
Disraeli's strategic speculations during the Eastern Question as
a mere Intelligence officer was as nothing compared to his
political and financial importance within the Liberal Party as a
member of the House of Baring and a nephew of Lord
Northbrook, a former Viceroy of India and Under-Secretary of
War and a future First Lord of the Admiralty? Finally, should
we adopt Michael Howard's more contemporary definition of
'statesmen' as being all those professional groups, including
soldiers, whose function it is 'to preserve and if necessary
exercise the power and authority of the State'?[12]

But here we must be careful, for the circumstances in which
soldiers exercise statesmanship or political authority, and the
manner in which they do so, have been organically conditioned
by the evolution of organised military and political
professionalism, within the General Staffs and party
associations respectively, as distinct, separate and increasingly
specialised functions within the State. We are often tempted
today to ascribe to the baroque and highly idiosyncratic
military politics of the eighteenth century those attributes of a
closed, disciplined, masonic corporation which only long
familiarity with the internal workings of a modern staff
headquarters or with the trendy jargon of military sociologists
could provide. There is a tendency to think of them in terms of

an inflexible, hierarchical Namier-like structure through which military interests and influence can be efficiently mobilised and decisively translated into civil authority and power. It was precisely to avert that eventuality and the coincidence of a second Cromwell that British military administration was organised to promote not tactical efficiency but the mutual interpenetrability of military and political society. For Cromwell had taught the British people that soldiers with too enthusiastic a conscience are as great a danger to the common liberty as those with no conscience at all. The purge of the Major-Generals had left them with a deep and ineradicable aversion to anything which conduced to arbitrariness in government.

They had solved, or at least shelved, their problem of the control of military power by virtually disbanding the standing army and distributing the responsibility for administering what rump remained among a wide range of agencies, boards, departments and committees, each saddled with vague and conflicting jurisdictions and answerable directly and separately to Parliament. In spite of the fact that throughout the eighteenth century Britain was almost continuously at war, there was no permanent Commander-in-Chief — an office and function personally wielded by the Hanoverian kings themselves in deference to if not ultimately in defence of their Continental preoccupations and interests — and no separate Secretaryship for War, like that for American affairs. Strategic policy was in the hands of two civilian Secretaries and the Master-General of Ordnance, usually the most illustrious soldier of the day who was also an honorary member of the Cabinet. Paradoxically, it was an unelected official, the Secretary-at-War, once the King's private military secretary, who controlled with the meticulous stringency usual to such an office the crucial purse-strings of military administration and finance. It was he who compiled and defended the annual estimates before the House without being in any way answerable to it, thereby avoiding any conflict of military with political interest. Before Lloyd, Pasley and Dundas, and indeed not until the Continental interpretations of Napoleonic warfare began to appear during the late 1820s, there was no conscious and cultivable sense of strategy as a function of national political institutions and ideas and subject in its application to a definable set of rational principles. There were no manoeuvres, no common and centrally regulated system of drills and evolutions; no clubs, canteens or societies, indeed none of the theory or machinery with which the armed forces of the Crown could achieve clear-cut and irrevocable decisions either in their politics at home or in their wars abroad.

For over two generations, therefore, Whig politicians had done all in their power, by institutionalising the anarchy of military administration and command, to prevent it from coalescing into a neo-Cromwellian threat to the State. The emergence of such machinery during the American and French Revolutionary Wars, as well as the contemporaneous examples of Washington and Napoleon, awakened fresh fears of Cromwellianism arising out of revolutionary contagion and industrial disorder. The establishment of military colleges, clubs, societies and institutes was evidence of a new permanently entrenched if unwelcome force in British politics and society, roughly approximating the recently incorporated technical professions of civil engineering and naval architecture. In the generation preceding the Crimean War this professional consciousness was to be fuelled and deepened by its own trade journals, by the flood of military memoirs and Alison's and Napier's histories of the Peninsular War, and by the publication of the despatches of England's greatest captains, Marlborough and Wellington.

But what troubled political society at large and the territorial aristocracy in particular was that this new and unpredictable military presence, if infiltrated by revolutionary agents, might transform itself into a revolutionary army which in league with radical Parliamentary forces would usurp and tyrannise the State — a fear that was by no means allayed by Wellington's becoming Prime Minister, insisting that he remain Commander-in-Chief, and when that failed taking into his Cabinet two of his veteran Peninsular officers. In these circumstances any office specifically set up for the better conduct of the war against Napoleon was construed as being raised for the duration only. In 1809, the independent Secretaryship of War, first formed in 1794, was merged with that of Colonies and rapidly found itself subordinated to that Ministry's overriding preoccupations with the economic and maritime aspects of administering the enlarged colonial Empire it had inherited after the Congress of

Vienna. The second volume of Sir Charles Pasley's pioneering study of the *Military Institutions and Policies of the British Empire* was suppressed because it advocated a war policy of increasing Continental commitments and an Imperial policy of the consolidation of British power in North America, Egypt and India. Frequent motions were made in the House to abolish the Staff College and a proposal to establish a separate Army Club was rejected by Parliament on the grounds that it was conducive to military conspiracy and sedition and would be allowed only if linked, like the combined Ministries of War and Colonies, to its apolitical and traditional ally, the Royal Navy. In the event, as might have been expected, Wellington refused to identify himself with the military clubs or with the interests of the Army as a whole. To have stirred up public agitation about the state of the Army against the Whigs whom he despised and who had long been obstructive would have been instantly misconstrued by Parliament and the country. As Master-General of Ordnance, Commander-in-Chief and Prime Minister, he presided over the virtual disintegration of the Army whose campaigns had made him the most famous soldier in Europe. He overruled the utilitarian recommendations of the Howicke Commission to consolidate the offices of Master-General of Ordnance and Commander-in-Chief under a civilian War Minister on the gounds that it would throw the Army into the radical hands of a dangerously enfranchised Parliament. Likewise, he stood firm against the Benthamite calls, common since Lloyd's day, to abolish purchase as the only way to preserve British society from the consequences of rival cliques of rootless professional soldiers, served only by their wits and their swords, who would pursue their advancement not in the patronage of the Crown but in the radical wings of the emerging political parties.[13]

All this, as mentioned before, was designed to prevent a second Cromwell arising in circumstances approximating those of civil war. And it was precisely because the reassertion of absolute military power in the manner of Cromwell in Ireland was as politically unthinkable as it was logistically impracticable a solution to the American rising of 1776 which, like the English Civil War before it and the Indian Mutiny after it, was recognised as a mixture of mutiny, rebellion, civil war and revolution and which admitted of no alternative solution save that of complete withdrawal, that the British conducted the war as half-heartedly and at such cross-purposes as they did.

The organisation of the Continental Army, like the constitutional provisions to ensure the close fusion of military office and political function, was modelled on eighteenth-century British practice, partly because in spite of the importation of foreign drill instructors it was the most familiar and readiest to hand and partly because a regular army, even though forced in the circumstances of its initial weakness and indiscipline to adopt Fabian tactics, was the best long-term guarantee of meeting and beating the British on their own terms in the field and at the conference table.[14] During the War of Independence, the Continental Army, which was often in the grip of mutiny, was inspected by half a dozen committees to test its political reliability. In 1782, a War Department was formed, headed by a Secretary-at-War whose functions, powers and jurisdictions with respect to the Commander-in-Chief, Congress or its French allies were left as vaguely defined as Washington's own. But just as General Benjamin Lincoln, the gouty and lethargic capitulator of Charleston, became the first head of the War Department, so did the mythology so vital to the life and purposes of the Revolution thrust upon Washington the combined attributes of a Great Captain and a Founding Father which a strict scholarly accounting of his military qualities and performance simply will not sustain. In the words of the most recent historian of the United States Army, 'he was to be a republican Soldier-President patterned upon the Royal Warrior of the European States,' or more specifically upon the kings and colonial governors of Hanoverian England whose function was as much to command armies in the field as to build an efficient administration at home or negotiate alliances abroad.[15] Moreover, military authority was to be shared between President and Congress, the American equivalents of King and Parliament, and military power between the Federal and State militias, their equivalents to the Armed Forces of the Crown and the county militias of Parliament. It is clear that the Constitution did not provide for a complete subordination of military power to political authority which most Americans have mistakenly taken for granted, but rather for the fusion of military office and political function which has allowed

American soldiers freer and more direct access to high political office than that enjoyed by their British counterparts, except in the government of Colonies or India. Henceforth after every major war, the doors of the White House have been open to its most successful generals: but especially to those who have been able to show that their flirtation with military greatness was merely part of a wider national adventure or crusade from which all would return to normality.[16]

This division of power and authority and the relationships and traditions which flowed from it were frozen, and until the Civil War forgotten, in the Constitution. Lacking the flexibility of the British situation, it could not be readily modified in the light of the emergence of professionalism in the conduct of politics and war and so would remain, as the Truman-MacArthur incident showed, a source of potential dispute and misunderstanding. No prominent British general, not even Haig or Montgomery, would have dared to challenge so openly his Prime Minister on a matter of strategic policy and expect the country to judge fairly between them. And when lesser generals did, from a misguided sense of patriotic duty, like Maurice in World War One, they acted in the full knowledge that they would be disowned by political and military superiors alike. Wellington has been the only professional soldier in modern British history to become Prime Minister, and his failure to satisfy expectations that he could produce in democratic politics the spectacular kind of victories which he had won in the field became a permanent reminder of Victorian 'political' generals that professional soldiers, however pre-eminent or powerful in their time, must as statesmen rule with a sword that is always too blunt, too short, or too inflexible to suit their purposes.

As integrity and the authority implicit in technical knowledge became one of the hallmarks of developing professionalism, few successful generals — no matter how strongly they might disapprove of the government's military policies or lack of them — dared risk compromising that by entering politics, though some like Wolseley were occasionally tempted or at least made calculated threats to do so. On the other hand, the British since Cromwell have always preferred their military heroes to be slightly scarred with failure, scandal or eccentricity, or best of all to die like Wolfe, Abercrombie or

Moore in the hour of victory, so that they would not have to live with the awkward and possibly dangerous consequences of exasperating military paragons. They expect of their generals an amateurish but obscure taste for literature, bird-watching or painting which, they trust, will modify the austere ideals of pure professionalism and mitigate the severity of their government should circumstances require that they exercise it. Allenby, Wavell and Slim, whose main achievements paradoxically lay in the East will always remain genuinely more representative of the British officer corps than Wellington, Haig or Montgomery. Moreover, though the British Army had never really been part of it, the age of the great captains had closed forever with Wellington's death: and as the revolutions in warfare, public administration and parliamentary government gathered force in the 1840s it was clear that British soldiers at least would no longer find the chance except perhaps in India or the colonies of obtaining by decisive victories that independent stature which had once been a passport for slipping into politics. In America, the Civil War brought to an end the era of the citizen-officer in presidential politics. Between 1880 and 1952 no professional soldier was nominated for the Presidency, although many had sought it.[17] So long as the balance of nuclear deterrence dominates what Michael Howard has rather oddly described as the Age of Peace,[18] it is unlikely that there will be another Eisenhower in the White House. Moreover, the development of Cabinet government in Britain made it decreasingly likely that a professional soldier, however skilled in battle and however broad his national appeal, could become Prime Minister. Carlyle's advice, that Wolseley should expel the House and set himself up as dictator, was idiosyncratic and, in the context of Victorian politics, despite a developing interest in the English Civil War on the part of the nascent historical profession[19] and in the American Civil War among British military intellectuals, such a view was not only unfashionable but totally impracticable.[20] None of the instruments of eighteenth-century military power, or the offices of its administration, had survived the successive invasions of predatory Victorian Parliaments. To the Crown, save only in the most ceremonial sense, none of its ancient military prerogatives remained. While Churchill, like Teddy Roosevelt, might use the Army and its small wars as a springboard into

politics, he was far from being a conventional professional
soldier. Yet as a politician, unlike Roosevelt, his military
outlook and unrepentant relish of war-mongering prevented
him from becoming Prime Minister until the drastically altered
circumstances of 1940 matched the man to his hour.

IV

By the end of the nineteenth century, the armies of the major
military powers of Europe and, to a lesser extent, those of
Britain and the United States had assumed the dominant
features of great corporations. The competing technical
requirements of their specialised components — intelligence,
the fighting arms and the commissariat — were composed
within a rigidly hierarchical structure of command according to
established codes of behaviour to achieve the basic purposes for
which they existed: instant obedience to higher political
direction and all-round instant war readiness. The utilitarian
ideals of Bentham, Jomini and Vigny which had prevailed since
the 1820s gave way after the great wars of the 1860s and 1870s
to the intoxicating Clausewitzian doctrines of the military
positivists at the Staff Colleges, who lectured a generation of
potential higher commanders that only through the acquisition,
consolidation and extension of its power in war could a nation's
integrity be maintained and its greatness be assured. For
almost a century theorists had defined the Army's functions in
metaphysical terms, as an almost abstract conception of
national power, without a significant life of its own, which
existed, like blocks on a sandtable, unmoved by the forces of
technical, social and political change.

Or so it seemed on the surface. For armies are composed of
men: some of great ability, ambition and no little cunning; men
who would reform the Army and perhaps the State in their own
image and who hold strong views about the purposes of an
Army and the policies which should be pursued to achieve
them. The drift from the institutionalised anarchy of the age of
the great captains to the corporate professionalism of that of
the General Staff inevitably generated within armies, especially
the British and American where it was freer to do so, a style and
pattern of politics of their own. A new breed of 'political' general
and his disciples emerged, who took it upon themselves to

voice, represent and realise 'military' interest — specific technical reforms or strategic policies — by aligning themselves quite shiftlessly as it suited their purposes with political parties holding or striving for power, or with radical groups within them. No longer able to rely on the victories which would decisively settle the outcome of a war in a single afternoon, these political generals and the cliques they led made the most of whatever commands they could engineer or which they could snatch from their rivals. At hand were the tools provided by the 'military enlightenment' which had burst so spontaneously, so brilliantly yet so briefly upon the major armies in the West between 1815 and 1854 — the trade journalism, clubs and societies. The era of wars of national consolidation and expansion in Europe, North America and some strategic points in the British Empire, starting with the Crimean War and ending with the Russo-Turkish War, called for more specialised agencies of military planning, education, intelligence and propaganda. The establishment of Staff Colleges, Intelligence Departments, military attachés, war correspondents, official histories and Cabinet Defence Committees provided ampler grounds for military politics and more subtle means to political generals for making their influence felt.

In Germany, the pressing needs of mass security and mass efficiency which had made her the foremost military power in Europe after 1870 meant that military thought and politics of a furtive or radical kind could not be allowed to flourish.[21] In so far as a state of military politics existed at all, the General Staff and its more hysterical protagonists such as Goltz and Bernhardi whose conception of the State was that of a super-General Staff, were its sole instrument and expression and were bound in the end and in an astonishing reversal of Clausewitz's classical dictum to take over the State itself. Indeed it is probably obvious that the virility of military politics is inversely proportionate to the monopolistic constraints inherent in a General Staff. In France, the potency and legitimacy of military politics suffered from its association with the humiliations of 1870. Thereafter, as Marshal MacMahon's Presidency and even more clearly the abortive Boulanger incident showed, in the fifteen years of intensive self-examination which followed those defeats, no French general or his following possessed the moral confidence or will-power to take over the Republic even when it was most vulnerable and submissive.[22] It was in Russia's conquest and administration of Central Asia, in America's pacification and settlement of the West, but above all in the shifting balance of Britain's strategic commitments towards the Indian Empire that the most vigorous conduct of military politics lay.

The objects of the new political generals were two-fold. By brisk and economical conduct of campaigns, and by their strong backing of technical military reforms and strategic policies (none of which necessarily contributed to the nation's security, power or prestige, but was useful to the electoral prospects of the party they then favoured), they tried to make themselves both politically indispensable and nationally popular. In return for this they might reasonably expect accelerated promotions or key appointments of their own choosing, and a greater share in the making of military policy. By circumventing in this way the traditional citadels of patronage, they became autonomous and to that degree rival citadels in their own right, but dispensing patronage of a more personal kind in which favouritism and loyalty counted for as much as efficiency, bravery or duty. Working this patronage for all it was worth, the political generals, within the strict confines of military society, aspired to influence and control only the *military* factor in the State, not the State itself. To secure command of these armies in wars which were small and few became the focal point of the Ringmanship which intensified and embittered the great strategic debates of the 1880s, and the even greater struggles for the Commanderships-in-Chief in Ireland, India and at the Horse Guards as they fell vacant in the 1890s. When such commands could not be contrived, they sought or would consider other paramilitary missions abroad, if certain prior conditions could be met and the prospects seemed bright.

But no political general worth his salt would accept out of a sense of duty a command or a commission which did not somehow increase his professional reputation and influence or put politicians in his debt. Wolseley's decision to accept the Lieutenant-Governorship of Natal in 1875 and the High Commissionership in Cyprus in 1878, like Roberts' anxiety to be appointed British representative to the Afghan Frontier Commission in 1885, are cases in point wherein the possibilities of a great Zulu or Russian war respectively were imminent.[23]

In order to make these campaigns, and the reforms which they might implicitly vindicate, appear to be more important than they were, or to discredit those of their rivals, the political generals would resort to all the journalistic tricks they could devise. These tricks included the suppression of despatches, the planting of false information with war correspondents, the closing or commandeering of the only usable telegraph line, the commissioning of official or unofficial histories of their campaigns and the calculated use of ghost-writers, leaks and after-dinner speeches — all designed to get to the public first with the most dramatic and authoritative accounting of their actions with which to forestall or disarm the criticism of their rivals.

Plots and counter-plots therefore became the very stuff of Victorian military politics and Wolseley — the model of the arch-*arriviste* whose advent Wellington had most feared but whose wide intellectual and literary tastes persuaded Henry James that he was the perfect 'specimen of the *cultured* British officer'[24] — was the most political and therefore fascinating general of the age. In all his dealings Wolseley was open, thrusting and shrewd. In comparison, Roberts, his closest rival in the business, was a mediocre functionary whose trivial campaigning experience and reforming efforts, having been paid for by the Indian Treasury, were rarely subject to the bracing criticism of Parliament or the press. If Wolseley had bound his career to the exigencies of Cardwell's Liberal reforms in the 1870s, Roberts conspired with the Conservative Opposition in the 1880s to become Commander-in-Chief in India and to press for the adoption of an Imperial defence strategy based on India rather than Britain. It was to vindicate Cardwell's reforms in action and the Eurocentric assumptions of British war policy on which they were based, as well as to strengthen his claims to the Indian Command (all-important in the event of a war against Russia in Central Asia), that Wolseley was prepared, as with Chelmsford in South Africa or Stephenson in Egypt, to supplant rival commanders. The Duke of Cambridge's alarm in 1879 that Wolseley and his Ring were secretly plotting with the Indian Government for Wolseley to become Commander-in-Chief of a localised Indian Army independent of Horse Guards' control might on the face of it seem no more than the paranoic anxiety of the Commander-in-Chief for the proprieties of his position: but whether malignantly engineered or not it was the closest thing to a drift towards Caesarism that the Victorian Age experienced and it was averted, not by the protests of the Queen, but by the timely and totally unexpected collapse of Disraeli's government and the recall of his impetuous Viceroy.[25]

But if empire-building created temptations for Caesarism that, for reasons which will be discussed later, were never attributed to Kitchener even at the height of his powers, it drained off any incipient tendencies towards civil war or militarism in government. The experience of vicarious dictatorship as Governors, especially in self-governing colonies while wars were brewing elsewhere, was a chastening one and extinguished any predilections they might have had for exercising the real thing. Ambitious military firebrands and political generals resented enforced or prolonged periods abroad administering colonies which effectually removed them from the centres of intrigue, reform and war-making and they tried, before setting out, to exact very specific and limited conditions of service which would not preclude instant and high command in a European war and their return to their old, or a higher, post in the War Office. But such terms were not always negotiable. Wolseley failed after returning from Natal in his attempts to bargain the offer of the Cape Governorship (which he did not want) against the guarantee by the Government that he would be given the chief command should war break out with China (which he did).[26] For in the give and take of military politics, the political generals discovered that in making themselves indispensable to politicians and political parties to achieve their military ends, they had unwittingly become the tools of party warfare. If they attracted too devoted a following in the country at large, were consistently outspoken or might otherwise prove an embarrassment at election times, they might find that their claims to an important field command had been denied, that they had been shelved in some remote colonial backwater or despatched on some particularly unsavoury errand from which their reputations might not emerge unimpaired. Thus Wolseley found himself a virtual political prisoner in Cyprus while wars were going badly in Afghanistan and South Africa. Only when they belatedly recognised that Wolseley alone could provide the kind of victories which could salvage their re-election prospects did the Conservatives unleash him to South Africa. But this was as far as they were prepared to go and they resisted the very considerable pressures, not least from Wolseley himself, that he be allowed to return to England or to assume the chief command in India. For much the same reason, Leonard Wood and Teddy Roosevelt were not given commands on the Western Front in 1917; Waldersee and Marchand were sent by their respective governments to China; MacArthur was shelved in the Pacific, and Wavell in India as Commander-in-Chief and Viceroy during and after the Second World War. Sometimes this was done to settle an old party grievance. In 1895, Wolseley's unchallengeable right to be Commander-in-Chief was overruled by the Liberals (who preferred Buller) because he had once threatened to resign as Adjutant-General and lead an Ulster Army against Home Rule. During World War One, General Gough was made a scapegoat for the German break-through in March 1918 by those who had never forgiven him for the part he had played in the Curragh 'mutiny' four years before. Roosevelt and Wood as Republicans were both denied overseas commands because, having criticised President Wilson's failure to declare war sooner, they stood vindicated and therefore a continuing embarrassment to the Democratic conduct of the war.[27]

Political parties could be particularly punishing or vindictive if generals did not live up to expectations in the field and by their victories save them from disaster at the polls. Soldiers, whether temporary Governors or long-term dictators, invariably organised and ran their colonies or their countries like military campaigns. Wolseley was no exception. Pressed for time, his eye cocked for more alluring possibilities elsewhere, yet ever watchful of envious critics, Wolseley's colonial policies, like his military victories, were meant to be sudden, decisive and dramatic. In imposing a truly 'Imperial' solution, he suborned the press, misled the war correspondents, intimidated or flattered the local opposition and rode rough-shod over much well-meant advice and sentiment. But in face of the complexities of colonial society and politics, such legalistic and doctrinaire settlements as he proposed could only be messy, inconclusive and short-lived, a lesson which was not lost on the Liberals — especially Hartington and Gladstone —

when they came to consider Wolseley's request for a dormant commission as Governor-General of the Sudan, should he require it to evict the intransigent Gordon from Khartoum. 'Excellent as Wolseley is as a general,' Gladstone is recorded as saying, 'he has not shown himself either in South Africa or Cyprus a good civil administrator.'[28] Even that military reputation for excellence did not survive the abortive if Homeric attempt to relieve Gordon's investment at Khartoum, and the long suppressed suspicions of Wolseley's legionary critics now bubbled over. They reminded a public shattered by news of Gordon's death that Wolseley's enemies (as at Red River or Kumasi) had rarely stood to fight, or that they had already been defeated (as in Zululand in 1879), or become undefeatable, as now, before his arrival at the decisive theatre of operations. Wolseley, they implied, was the very last man even under the most favourable circumstances to have saved Gordon. He had only fought one real battle — at Tel el Kebir — and even there he had been dragged back from the brink of disaster by the imaginative intervention of Hamley's Highland Division, something which Wolseley had attempted to conceal in the official despatches and history.

It is almost certain that had Wolseley relieved Khartoum, Gladstone's government would not have fallen.[29] But in the failure to do so, the relationship between the political generals and the political parties, which had always been one of mutual convenience, was broken forever. Military politicians such as Colonel F.A. Stanley, Hugh Childers and Lord Carnarvon, who had always sympathised with Wolseley's notions of British war policy and colonial defence, gave way to those self-made strategists of Indian defence such as Joseph Chamberlain, Sir Charles Dilke and Lord Randolph Churchill, who most emphatically did not. Thereafter no government, liberal or conservative, would trust as unreservedly as they had done in Wolseley's strategic advice or generalship. Moreover, Wolseley had been indiscreet enough to admit that, given the chance, he would precipitate a great European war so that he might be called upon as Supreme War Lord or virtual military dictator, as Kitchener was in 1914. Such a confession, taken with Wolseley's unguarded threats about Ulster, was probably enough to convince the Liberal Government that it ought not to take any chances by appointing Wolseley to the chief command in the Empire. It was Kitchener, therefore, and not Wolseley, who achieved Wolseley's most precious ambitions: to become Commander-in-Chief in India, to reform the Indian Army, and to become Minister of War in the great European war he prayed would come in his time. It is interesting to speculate why, considering Kitchener's technical background, his ignorance of the British Army, British politics and British public opinion, and his comparatively limited range of campaigning experience, he was appointed to such a position.

Unnerved and shaken by the Khartoum débâcle and what it had done to his reputation and influence, Wolseley began to insist that the only way to dig the Army out of the rut of party politics into which he, above all others, had led it, was to make the Commander-in-Chief *ex officio* Minister of War. As the permanent unelected war member of the Cabinet in whatever government was in office, he would present to the country through Parliament an annual and expert statement of the military conditions and needs of the Empire and leave it to the people to decide whether and how they were to be met.[30] It was, in a sense, a return to the honorific eighteenth-century status of the Master-General of Ordnance, with whom Wolseley, engaged upon writing his *Life of Marlborough*, probably identified himself. But such an arrangement presupposed that the collective intelligence of the country would be more enlightened and responsive than that of a civilian War Minister, that it could be more easily captured in respect of military deficiencies by generals than by civilian Cabinet Ministers and that generals can persuade masses better than Ministers and politicians. It also pre-supposed that elected governments would be so foolish as to place themselves in the hands of a soldier who by fudging a few figures or by some off-hand remark had it in his power to turn the country against them. And it pre-supposed what no rational Victorian before the South African War would accept, that defence was or ought to be a central concern of governments and peoples.

Why was it therefore that a Liberal Government was prepared to accord to Kitchener in 1914 powers which it had denied Wolseley scarcely ten years before? Was it simply that Wolseley had for too long been too close to the centre of affairs and was bound to lose the credibility which only detachment and a certain hauteur could maintain? Or was it that in the

Sudan Kitchener had been permitted what Wolseley, because of the exigencies of the Penjdeh Crisis, had been forbidden to do: to avenge Gordon's death with a dramatic and decisive demonstration of force. As the Royal Engineer who had compiled the Official Report on the Fall of Khartoum in 1885, Kitchener had also been chosen to command the Expedition against Wolseley's express advice. Or was it that in South Africa Kitchener had brought to a just and sane conclusion a war for which Wolseley as Commander-in-Chief had been partly responsible? Or were the causes deeper and more complex? Did they lie perhaps in the calibre of the politicans with whom each had to deal? Or was it due to the new strategic circumstances brought about by the South African War, the Japanese defeat of Russia and the naval threat of Germany which revolutionised public and official attitudes towards defence planning and preparation?[31]

Victorian small wars were not fought in the direct defence of Britain's shores or of her strategic interest in the Low countries and therefore obviated the need for a Cromwellian approach to defence administration, which seemed appropriate only to India, the heart of Imperial power, which would bear the chief burden and become the centre of strategic gravity of any great war against Russia. But the likelihood of that war, which had obsessed a generation of Indian strategists, visibly diminished at the hands of Japan, and the strategic reasoning behind the Indian commitment seemed irrelevant to the more urgent question of the defence of England against Germany. It was, therefore, perhaps natural that politicians should turn in their hour of need to the soldier who had most effectively organised India's defences when India rather than England had seemed the closest and most likely object of an enemy invasion.

It became fashionable after Wolseley's death for his admirers to claim that he had never been really stretched or tested in the battles of a great war, but that if he had he would have acquitted himself better than that generation of Edwardian commanders which included Kitchener, Haig and Ian Hamilton, who had been groomed in the steamy stables of his detractor, Lord Roberts. We cannot tell. He would have preferred command of the Expeditionary Force to administration of the War Office. His French was passable, but he did not like Frenchmen and had expected at some time during his career to go to war with them. In manner he was more elegant and compliant than Kitchener; in debate more vigorous but more wordy. He understood as neither Kitchener nor Wellington before him did the the conditions of continental warfare and the temper of British politics. His grasp of logistics was exhaustive. His judgement of men was generally sound, though sometimes flawed by favouritism. Unlike Kitchener, who virtually destroyed the Indian General Staff and scrapped the War Office mobilisation plans, Wolseley drafted his master plan and expected his military cabinet of diverse, luminous talents to put it into effect. What his real ceiling was we shall never know.

V

The mutual contempt felt by generals and politicians as a result of the Curragh 'mutiny' and Kitchener's deplorable management of the War Office, intensified by the strategic disputes of the last three years of the War, brought to a close the Victorian phenomenon of the self-made, freelance political general. He had never flourished or enjoyed much prominence on the Continent, and though British generals would continue to govern colonies overseas, they were to do so in the drastically reduced circumstances of Britain's imperial and military decline. They often found themselves, in an ironic and realistic appreciation of their difficulties, bowing to local nationalist pressures which would have horrified Wolseley, as it did Churchill and all those romantics in the inter-war years who maintained their Victorian convictions that Empires were still ruled by swords, even when the will and the capacity to draw them had been exhausted.

The demands of National Government in total coalition warfare called as never before for the closest co-ordination of military, economic and foreign policies and for the development of a new breed of 'soldier-statesman', remarkable as much for his political and diplomatic skills as for his strictly military expertise and advice. Michael Howard has alleged that the 'Anglo-American military leader of the mid-twentieth century' was 'as skilled at organising a service in a complex team of varied talents and nationalities as any business operative or political boss': but the emphasis must distinctly be placed upon the word American. Of this new breed Robertson and Allenby were pioneers rather than prototypes; for however much they might despise those 'modern Major-Generals' who scuttled home before finishing off their wars, or those like Haig and Henry Wilson who indulged in a particularly malicious form of intrigue, the scope for strategic statesmanship, it if could be exercised at all, was confined to the arid campaign on the Western Front and its marginally more fruitful sideshows in the colonial Middle East and Africa. Although the proximity of this campaign theatre and the lack of any constitutional provision or precedent more recent than the Civil War left the American Government unable to restrict the strategic independence of its generals overseas as purposefully as Lloyd George was curbing his, neither Robertson nor Allenby enjoyed after four years of war the degree of political responsibility which the prickly and inexperienced Pershing did after four months. But it is worth noting that Wavell, who was the only soldier to work closely with both of them during the First World War, became as the first soldier-Viceroy of India the greatest British soldier-statesman of the Second.

In Britain between the wars the inculcation of skills and attitudes appropriate to the new role of soldier-statesman became one of the functions of the Imperial Defence College. But the real reasons for the wartime proliferation of soldier-statesmen lay elsewhere. Most obviously they resulted from the more complex and varied strategic nature of the Second World War. But most of all they lay in the rise of American military power and in the inscrutable processes of the American military tradition which allowed the fusion of military office and political function. The conduct of war was regarded, not with the pragmatism of the British, but as a bizarre combination of crusade and business. These were the conditions which produced, with quite astonishing fertility and regularity, the soldier-statesmen who were to organise and manage not only the combined strategy of the Grand Alliance but also the post-war administration of occupied Germany and Japan. Equipped with the plenipotentiary powers of Foreign Ministers and Ambassadors Extraordinary, American soldiers

rather than politicians conducted America's wartime relations
with the Free French, the Republican and Nationalist Chinese
and the British Dominions.[32] Eisenhower personally
negotiated the surrender of Italy and MacArthur and Clay
became virtual dictators of conquered Japan and Germany
respectively. It was on the face of it an extraordinary display of
military predominance in political judgement on the part of a
nation which had always managed to persuade itself that it was
unmilitary.

On the other hand, no British general — not even Wavell as
he grappled with the combined political, diplomatic and
administrative difficulties of Greece, Crete, Turkey, Syria and
Ethiopia between 1940 and 1941 or the problems presented by
Indian nationalism between 1943 and 1947 — shared or even
sought quite the same latitude of political independence. It was
Wavell who first suggested the setting up of a War Council or
Cabinet Sub-Committee to relieve him of these problems in the
Middle East.[33] Moreover, no general, however pre-eminent or
victorious, could have long remained immune from the prying
interventions of the Prime Minister who, as Minister of Defence
working in close and continuous contact with his professional
Service Chiefs, had equipped himself with powers for
conducting war unprecedented in British history. Yet where
soldiers did exercise supreme authority — Clay in Germany,
MacArthur in Japan and Wavell in India — they did so with a
depth of compassion and an understanding of local difficulties
which was totally opposed to the short shrift those countries
would have received at the hands of some American and British
politicians. Both Clay and MacArthur successfully resisted
demands from within the State Department, the Treasury and
Congress to inflict a Carthaginian peace; while Wavell
stubbornly insisted, despite Churchill's frequent and disloyal
outbursts, that the explosive issue of Indian independence
could not and would not be shelved until the end of the war.[34]
It is likely that much of the antipathy between Churchill and
Wavell was caused by Churchill's exclusive preoccupation with
the practical matter of winning the war and his inability to see
the logistical, moral and Imperial implications of that objective.
Churchill preferred simpler soldiers like Montgomery who were
not troubled by such matters and fired those — and the list is a
long one — who were.

These, then, were the conditions of soldiers enjoying unprecedented and extra-constitutional degrees of political power without presuming, even in De Gaulle's case, to take over the State by force, from which the classical criteria and stereotypes of military professionalism were deduced. But quite obviously such criteria and stereotypes cannot be applied to soldiers who become heads of State during wars or revolutions, when the existence or legitimacy of the State is in dispute. Indeed any discussion of soldiers-as-statesmen must start by distinguishing clearly between the soldier as a natural political animal — his personality, beliefs and attitudes — and the soldier as a member of a profession whose ideals and doctrines he discards or exploits in his exercise of supreme political power. In the more mature states of the West, soldiers who have become statesmen, including the subjects of the present studies, have rarely if ever done so in the name of their profession or to establish a praetorian state. Despite their rank and experience they might be said to have been in the Army but not of it. Throughout De Gaulle's earliest writings, for instance, there runs a tremor of mutinous discontent with and calculated insubordination to the anonymous pusillanimity of contemporary French politics which would never have attained its prophetic significance had he been politically 'assassinated', as Roosevelt and Churchill wished, during the war.[35] More alive than other professions to the importance of tradition and prestige when that is most needed, the classical soldier-turned-statesman will put the State above the Army, the nation above the government, and develop an almost mystical identification with a Higher Order on whose behalf he will claim to act. Thus we have Cromwell in the name of his Conscience, Wellington and Washington in that of a rational Constitution and De Gaulle in that of 'une certaine idée de la France'. In his hands, the conservative characteristics of the military profession — sense of mission, order, efficiency and identity — will be transformed into a positive and sometimes revolutionary force for national rejuvenation: to give back the State its moral belief in itself and its will to thrive. No one can understand Franco or De Gaulle who ignores the impact of the loss of the Spanish Empire in the war against America in 1898 upon the former,[36] or that of the defeat of France in 1940 upon the latter. The soldier-as-statesman incarnated 'something primordial, permanent and necessary' — the sovereignty or virtue of the State: its traditions, mystique, power and capacity to reclaim or reassert from within itself conditions indispensable to its existence and growth. These conditions could vary according to the particular circumstances of the State, in independence, unity, order, stability and self-respect; or, as De Gaulle saw it, 'resurrection, reconstruction and renovation'. He must be 'part Legislator, part Roman dictator, part Prince' and must act, in Stanley Hoffman's phrase, 'like a whole political class'.[37] The central problem posed by the phenomenon of soldier as chief of state, therefore, is this: to what extent and in what ways can the ideals and attitudes which soldiers and politicians find exclusively repellent be made mutually reinforcing and transformed into statesmanship? Each case will be unique and the manner in which the soldier perceives the incarnate State will vary according to its political traditions and institutions as well as to its immediate circumstances and needs. Our choice of the subjects of these studies was deliberately restricted to the twentieth century for two reasons: there seemed a greater likelihood that the 'modern Major-Generals' would be just that, full-blooded professional soldiers in the best Cromwellian sense: and because such soldiers made our central concern — the nature and properties of the dialectic between military professionalism and statesmanship — that much more explicit and manageable.

Why is it, for instance, that almost invariably we expect such soldiers to seize the State by the throat in the name of some mystical professional imperative and ride rough-shod over the rule of law and the popular will when in most cases they do not? Why do we expect of them a code of behaviour and an approach to state-craft less beneficial to the State than those of lawyers or businessmen? Victorian generals believed that the civilian professions — men of trading, religious or legalistic instincts — were incapable of appreciating the limitations and potentiality of armed power in international or imperial politics and therefore of resolving the gritty and often dirty problems of war and peace. It is probably safe to say that soldiers would have stood up to the dictators in the 1930s more readily and courageously than Baldwin or Chamberlain. Certainly Franco and Pétain were eventually to do so in less advantageous circumstances. To what extent therefore can and does the soldier-as-statesman use the mystique of the armed forces to maintain himself in power, and is there a point, as De Gaulle once believed, beyond which the prolongation of patrimonial rule becomes counter-productive? Does the soldier-as-statesman tend to place too great a weight upon the strategic factor in national policy or because he personifies it to take it for granted and therefore forget it? Does he bring into government old military habits or methods or even friends, secretive and conspiratorial, which might alienate his colleagues and the public and cut him off from the fresh ideas of young men who should be given their heads? How does he maintain the loyalty of the Army without allowing it to become sufficiently powerful to overthrow him? Not all of these questions could be asked of every case and each would have to be answered according to the circumstances.

VI

Not all soldiers instinctively sought, especially in democratic societies, to impose authoritarianism upon the State or to identify themselves too closely with the armed forces whose servitude and grandeur they had recently endured. Of the military reputations of the great captains — Cromwell, Napoleon and Wellington — there can be no question. Allenby was described by his pupil and successor in the Middle East, Wavell, in a biography which is as revealing of the author as its subject, as 'the best British General of the Great War'.[38] Both were cast in the Wellingtonian mould, dry, courteous, with a share of common sense, lacking the divine spark and the common touch, but believing that sound administration was the basis of all good strategy and clean warfare. Franco was successively the youngest captain, colonel and general in the Spanish Army, its leading intellectual, a profound student of Napoleon, as famous for his command of the Spanish Legion as for his Directorship of the Zaragoza Military Academy.[39] Even Eisenhower, whose reputation was that of a managing rather than a fighting general, had risen astonishingly rapidly in the short American months of World War One, as he was to do again in World War Two under the patronage of Marshall.[40]

The best soldiers have usually been most alive to the changing military technology of their times: it was true of

Franco and Wavell and even of De Gaulle and Eisenhower who, though neither would command in action anything greater than a regiment, were both reprimanded for publishing lectures in support of mechanised warfare. But rank and reputation of a strictly military kind do not in themselves guarantee a smooth and rapid path to high political office; nor on the other hand does a truculent refusal to conform to the norms and disciplines of the profession of arms necessarily imply a greater aptitude for statecraft. De Gaulle was never tested in high command and would have been a difficult if not impossible subordinate. As a field commander, Washington was not tested often enough, or on a large enough scale, to be ranked automatically alongside Napoleon or Wellington.[41] His practical experience was confined to the raiding operations of 'la petite guerre'. Like Eisenhower, his first-hand knowledge of the technical branches of the Army was extremely slight: he had never commanded a cavalry unit, employed massed artillery or administered rear base installations of any size. He shifted the blame for his mistakes upon others, suspected a conspiracy to unseat him and took criticism badly. He placed himself too much in the hands of his staff and 'never once defeated the enemy's main army in a major engagement in the open field'. British generalship was so hesitant and mediocre and French assistance so decisive that it is impossible to determine Washington's own *military* contribution to the outcome. But then he was chosen Commander-in-Chief for political, not military reasons — to weld the States together into an effective *national* resistance, co-operate with the French, reconcile the competing claims of different theatres of war and negotiate the British surrenders — just as he later became President because he above all embodied the dispassionate and intrinsic virtues of the new State. Marcus Cunliffe was probably correct when he said that of all the historical parallels that could be drawn, Washington best combined the managerial talents for coalition warfare of Eisenhower with the charismatic purposefulness and vision of De Gaulle.[42] Where soldiers, however capable as generals, fail to incarnate the essential spirit and purpose of the State, they rapidly become mere figureheads, unable to sustain their legitimacy and liable to be swept aside by forces they do not understand.

Because soldiers as chiefs of state in democratic countries

have been conscious of representing a constituency higher than
that of the armed forces, they have been reluctant, at least since
Cromwell's day, to use those forces to enforce or extend their
mandate. Washington may have been thoughtless in accepting
the Presidency of the Society of Cincinnati which was dedicated
to perpetuating the Revolutionary Officer Corps through
heredity and therefore smacked of aristocratic counter-
revolution, but 'he made it plain beyond doubt that he
cherished no overweening dream of military dictatorship.'[43]
Likewise, Wellington, with whom he was often compared,
refused to lend his name or support to the military clubs, the
colonels' lobby in Parliament or the case for reform. On the
other hand, he created the Metropolitan Police Force which in
times of crisis might be interposed between the constitution
and those radical groups in the Army and the country at large
who might seek to overthrow it. As a youthful witness of the
Curragh affair, Wavell wrote to his father in dismay and
exasperation: 'What right have the Army to be on the side of
the Opposition, what have they to do with causing the fall of
Government?'[44] Over the next thirty years his views did not
change. When it was jokingly and anonymously put to him at a
bad time of the war, when many were questioning Churchill's
judgement and leadership but when he personally was riding on
the crest of his Italian victories, that he might become more
easily than he imagined a second Cromwell, he replied with
characteristic modesty: 'Myself (since you have mentioned me
as a White Hope) — quite small table beer, I am afraid: a good
journeyman soldier who knows his job reasonably well, not
afraid of responsibility but not seeking it; quite intelligent for
one of the Unintelligentsia; confident enough in his normal
judgement of things military: but no divine fire for leadership
of a people. So that's that.'[45] Even Franco did not establish a
military dynasty or exact of his Army an oath of personal
allegiance to himself. As President, Eisenhower took deliberate
pains to keep the soldier in his place or at least at arm's length.
He increased the countervailing powers of the civilian Secretary
of Defense, took decisions without consulting the Joint Chiefs,
refused to become embroiled in a full-scale Asian war, presided
over the demobilisation of the post-Korean Army and pointed
an admonitory finger at the sinister implications of the
military-industrial basis of American nuclear power whose

functioning he himself barely understood and whose growth he had been powerless to contain.[46] Unlike Kitchener (or his Canadian parody, Colonel Sam Hughes) who even as Minister of War felt that his authority and prestige both in Cabinet and in the field would be demeaned or weakened if he did not wear his Field Marshal's uniform, and unlike Churchill who shifted theatrically among a variety of uniforms and costumes, De Gaulle never assumed in his public dress a rank higher than that of the Brigadier-General he was. In spite of the fact that his authority rested to an extraordinary degree upon the 'might, magic and mystery of words', he never 'encouraged a personality cult' or 'sought to perpetuate his system'. Although he wrote of the temptations and the occasional value of a temporary dictatorship, he never envisaged a *coup d'état* against the Fourth Republic. 'No man', he wrote, 'can substitute himself for a people.'[47]

This is not to say that something of his military temperament and training will not infiltrate his style and methods of government. After all, the soldier-statesman is born in war and revolution and military power is intrinsic to the sovereignty of the State he purportedly incarnates. The degree and manner in which this is allowed to manifest itself publicly in the conduct of affairs, however, will vary according to the practical needs of the moment — unity, stability, reconstruction, modernisation or whatever — consistent with his perception of the sovereign and moral purposes of the State and his capacity to synthesise and project them in terms of its past. Few soldiers who become chiefs of state will not have prepared themselves in some sort of way, in drab years of peace or in the course of war, by chance or by design, intellectually, psychologically or practically, for the statesmanship of high command. Some, such as Washington, Wellington and Eisenhower, by their management of wartime and post-war diplomacy, had made their claims to supreme political office as inevitable and indisputable as they were unpremeditated. Others in circumstances of declining military power, defeat or civil war, have formulated long before they have attained rank or power a revolutionary or at least revitalised conception of the sort of State they might wish to construct and personify. Still others will content themselves with the modest and, as sometimes happens, prophetic exploration of the relationship between generals and politicians, of the qualities of the ideal Higher Commander, or of a soldier functioning as a statesman in a subordinate colonial setting.

Ataturk, for instance, had been deeply impressed with H.G. Wells's doctrine of scientific and material determinism[48] which Wavell, sympathetic though he was to the aspirations of Indian nationalism, was sufficiently knowledgeable of human nature, government and administration to see through as 'sheer nonsense . . . inaccurate history and unpractical social theories' upon which no State, least of all an Asian State without settled traditions of independent democratic practice, could be lastingly constructed.[49] Nasser modelled himself not upon Ataturk and the socialist modernisers of the Kemalist revolution but upon General Aziz Ali al Misri, 'the father of the Arab nationalist movement and the revolutionary leader *par excellence* who championed the Arab cause against Turkish domination.' From 1919 onwards he became the model of all Arab officers: 'heroic, quarrelsome, arrogant, a desperado and political acrobat, constantly plotting, never loyal to men, régimes or ideologies, but rather to the advancement of his personal career, the military, and primitive slogans of militarism and of course to romantic nationalism' — the precursor of contemporary Arab military praetorians, a reincarnation of Byzantine power and intrigue and Islamic authoritarian tradition.[50]

During the inter-war years, both De Gaulle and Wavell had unwittingly equipped themselves as future statesmen in roles which neither could then have foreseen. In his Royal United Service Institute lecture on the Higher Commander, in his Lees Knowles' lectures on generals and generalship, in his study of the Palestine campaign, but especially in his biography of Allenby as a soldier and statesman — the most self-revealing and prophetic of all his books — Wavell had intellectually equipped himself for the problems he would face in Palestine, the Middle East and India as completely as Churchill's writing of his monumental biography of Marlborough had fitted him to cope with the coalition problems of World War Two.[51] De Gaulle's case is more complex and less concrete. Writing at the floodtide of the post-war period of literary disenchantment, when the French Army was reorganised on a peace footing, De Gaulle's disenchantment was of a different kind: he was irascible and prickly, the anonymity and impotence of his place as an obscure servant of contemptible French politics rankled badly; his dissatisfaction was levelled not at the illustrious past but at the drab and unheroic present. In his prophecies of future grandeur, his romantic glorification of war, his impatient conception of politics as the realm of the instinctual and contingent, and his notion of the Army as the true soul of a nation, even in his second-hand ideas about mechanised warfare, De Gaulle combined the melancholic traditions of Guibert and Vigny.

While the formal and traditional procedures of democratic politics, or at least the hypocrisy, evasiveness and dishonesty which passes for such, often strikes the soldier as contemptible and ineffectual, he often has a surer sense of power, a less alarmist disposition towards intelligence of enemy intentions and capabilities, and a more realistic appreciation of the importance of moderation in the conduct of international and imperial diplomacy. It was Wellington who insisted that France should not be permanently dismembered and humiliated, as Britain's Continental allies wished, by the annexation of the Low Countries and by the establishment of an international 'Army of Observation' at Brussels.[52] Wavell's courageous and unrequited stand as Viceroy in dragging the Churchill and Attlee governments to face the matter of Indian independence squarely and honestly, whether it was politically inconvenient or not, is a more interesting case in point.[53]

It has already been mentioned that Wavell was a close student and admirer of Allenby's progressive and liberal statesmanship in Palestine and Egypt; and it was therefore significant that the second volume of his biography of Allenby, which dealt sympathetically with Allenby's position as High Commissioner on Egyptian independence, should have been published shortly after he had accepted Churchill's invitation to go to India as Viceroy. Churchill's motives in appointing Wavell whom he considered a burnt-out soldier and an embarrassment to his allies were two-fold: to shelve Wavell's unacceptable but otherwise indisputable claims to be Supreme Commander in the Far East and therefore his chance of redeeming his defeatist reputation in the Middle East; and to keep things quiet in India, as a stop-gap Viceroy who could be safely ignored until the war ended. But in ridding himself of a

military embarrassment, Churchill created an even greater
political one. For in his biography Wavell had reminded the
world that although Allenby 'had a better knowledge and
instinctive understanding of the complex political problems
of the Middle East than any member of the British Cabinet',[54]
he had been summarily squeezed out of the High Commission
by the Churchill faction because in its view Allenby's
progressive attitudes threatened to destabilise the former
Ottoman — now British — Empire in the Middle East as an
outwork to the defences of India. These untimely revelations
came as a great shock to Churchill who almost refused to attend
the Cabinet's farewell dinner to Wavell on the eve of his
departure to India. Nothing could have been better calculated
to worsen the already strained relations between Churchill and
his Viceroy-elect whose run of adversity had not dimmed his
awkward streak of integrity and independence and whose dour
taste for logistics while Commander-in-Chief in the Middle East
seemed, at least from Churchill's point of view, to have taken all
the fun and glamour out of war. Wavell believed that Churchill
for his part now resented and regretted having made an
appointment he could not countermand. For the next four
months, as the transfer of Vice-regal power was completed, he
taunted Wavell relentlessly about the political unreliability of
the Indian Army which Wavell had recently commanded. 'He
accused me of creating a Frankenstein by putting modern
weapons in the hands of sepoys,' wrote Wavell, 'spoke of 1857,
and really was almost childish about it. I tried to reassure
him . . . but he has a curious complex about India and is always
loath to hear good of it and apt to believe the worst. He has still
at heart his cavalry subaltern's idea of India, just as his
military tactics are inclined to date from the Boer War. . . . He
hates India and everything to do with it.'

Amery told Wavell that Churchill knew 'as much of the
Indian problem as George III did of the American Colonies.' As
Wavell saw it, Churchill feared that any fresh political advance
in India, especially in the midst of a great war, would split the
Conservative Party and turn the House against him.[55] It
would also seem a concession to American public opinion which
for some time had been demanding that as a *quid pro quo* for
increased American military co-operation Britain should
promptly allow India to become an independent republic of

united states. But it was a concession which Churchill for reasons of British prestige could and would not admit. All this, according to Wavell, was mere politics, not statesmanship, and for the next four unhappy years he pursued his self-appointed task of bringing Churchill's government to an honest and honourable appreciation of its constitutional obligations to India. Whereas in the Western Desert Churchill had forced Wavell's pace, now the shoe was on the other foot. Churchill retaliated with abusive prejudice, prevarication and implied charges that Wavell, once again, was unable to keep the enemy from the gates. It must be stated in fairness to Churchill, however, that the Labour Government, from whom Wavell might reasonably have expected more sympathy with his objectives of a swift and generous settlement, did not treat Wavell much better. Indeed it treated him a great deal worse, for it totally misunderstood the kind of soldier he was and went behind his back to deal directly with the leaders of the Congress Party. All Wavell's hopes of a united, stable and friendly India as the best bulwark to British prestige and security in the East were thereby forever dashed. Few generals in British history have deserved better of their politicians than Wavell.

For the soldier returning as statesman, too much continuous service abroad can become a positive handicap in coming to terms with the partisan tempo of domestic politics. Wellington for instance never understood the growing importance of public opinion, especially in a reformed Parliament, and the need to capture and cater to it. That was tantamount to demagoguery and next door to mutiny. Like Kitchener a hundred years later, he did not know England and between 1784 and 1818 had rarely lived there. He did not know Parliament, especially the Commons: he did not know the Army, had never identified himself with the common soldiery and his relations with the War Office had been singularly cool. As Sir Walter Scott and most political and military historians have agreed, India, Spain and Dublin Castle was the wrong education for British leadership at a time of democratic aspiration: and Wellington became, in the words of C.R.M.F. Cruttwell, 'the worst Prime Minister of the nineteenth century'.[56] The day-to-day practice of politics soldiers often find uncongenial and distasteful: a bizarre blend of sainthood and charlatanry. Trained to take and implement decisions, they dislike making them 'in the sticky and unpleasant heat' of endless political discussion.

Lushington spoke for most soldiers when he said of Wellington that he lacked the capacity for explaining and supporting measures in debate. His delivery was inelegant, disjointed and unpractised and yet somehow his arguments converged, as his battles had done, to a single decisive point. Roberts was fond of saying that whenever Wolseley got to his feet he lost his head. But that was sour grapes. Wolseley could be an effective speaker when he chose to be: but he found it degrading as well as pointless to waste his breath upon a pack of shifty, evasive and ineffectual politicians and preferred to put his case on paper, either in the form of an official memorandum or more controversially in that of a published article. Kitchener and Haig were reputed to have conversed in agricultural grunts and Wavell, in words which applied as much to himself, likened Allenby's mind to a battleship, powerful and weighty, but requiring time and space to turn and manoeuvre. Alanbrooke's mind and delivery, on the other hand, has been likened to a machine gun. What was so astonishing, so totally unlooked-for from his dark, smouldering, disdainful presence, no matter whom he was addressing — the Cabinet, the Prime Minister, visiting Ministers or Commanders, the American Chiefs of Staff — was 'the speed with which the words issued forth, as rapid as machine-gun fire, a prolonged burst and then a breath fetched hastily with a sort of indrawn groan and then another unchecked burst':

. . .the boldest might quail before this onslaught and many did . . .. It was frightening, this direct assault, and it was sometimes incomprehensible. The words tumbled over each other and any words that came to hand were fired off indiscriminately. Germans became Russians, Americans became Japanese, Rome found itself in Egypt and Cairo on the Persian Gulf, Montgomery was defending Stalingrad and Stalin sitting in the White House. The combinations were to be read out aloud by the CIGS. Whole lines were omitted and it required a lot of imagination to supply the gaps. But there was never any question of taking advantage of these strange slips of memory or quirks of interpretation. If you had dared to interrupt with a demure and smug 'Sir, do you mean Germans — or do you mean

Alamein?' you would have been blasted out of the room.[57]

The sheer violence and speed of Alanbrooke's thoughts confounded his opposition or sent it running for cover. But that can be said of few generals, especially those who must work within the peacetime constraints of statesmanship. Sensing the futility of political argument, by temperament and professional habit reclusive if not secretive in methods of work, seeking not merely decisions but a clear and public record of them, soldiers often do better closeted behind a desk with pen and paper than free-wheeling in public debate. Sometimes this can give an unfortunate impression of cold indifference, or of being a lack-lustre figurehead in the hands of others. Wellington, Wolseley, Haig, Robertson, Slim and Wavell all respected the power of the written word and, unlike most American or Canadian generals, were accomplished in its use. But of all the Western soldier-statesmen in the twentieth century only De Gaulle seemed to have much aptitude or liking for oratory; in his hands, it has been said, television became the absolute weapon of the Fifth Republic.[58]

NOTES

1. W.E.K. Anderson (ed.), *The Journal of Sir Walter Scott* (Oxford, Clarendon, 1972), p. 208. The entry is for 8 October 1826.
2. Lester E. Pearson, *Mike: the Memoirs of . . .* (Toronto, University of Toronto Press, 1972), vol. I p. 165.
3. See Michael Howard's introduction, 'The Armed Forces as a Political Problem', to his edited collection of lectures, *Soldiers and Governments: Nine Studies in Civil-Military Relations* (London, Eyre and Spottiswoode, 1957), p. 13. These views he modified slightly in 'Civil-Military Relations in Great Britain and the United States, 1945-58', *Political Science Quarterly*, LXXV, March 1960, p. 36.
4. See for instance R. Pinkney, 'The Theory and Practice of Military Government', *Political Studies*, XXI, No. 2, pp. 152-66; E.A. Nordlinger, 'Soldiers in Mufti: the Impact of Military Rule upon Economic and Social Change in the Non-Western states', *American Political Science Review*, vol. 64, 1970, pp. 1131-48.
5. For instance, Brian Crozier, *Franco: A Biographical History* (London, Eyre and Spottiswoode, 1967); *De Gaulle, The Statesman* (London, Eyre Methuen, 1973); Lord Kinross, *Ataturk: the Rebirth of a Nation* (London, Cassell, 1965); John Connell, *Wavell, Soldier and Scholar* (London, Collins, 1964); Elisabeth Longford, *Wellington: Pillar of State* (London, Widenfeld and Nicolson, 1972); Sir Edward Spears, *Two Men Who Saved France: Pétain and De Gaulle* (London, Eyre and Spottiswoode, 1966); Antonia Fraser, *Cromwell: Our Chief of Men* (London, Weidenfeld and Nicolson, 1973); A.P. Wavell, *Allenby, Soldier and Statesman* (London, Constable, 1944).
6. S.P. Huntington, *The Soldier and the State: The Theory and Politics of Civil-Military Relations* (New York, Knopf, 1957); M. Janowitz, *The Professional Soldier, A Social and Political Portrait* (New York, Free Press, 1964).
7. J.E. Smith (ed.), *The Papers of General Lucius D. Clay: Germany, 1945-9* (Bloomington, Indiana University Press, 1974).
8. Much of the credit for this must go to Russell Weigley whose output and perhaps influence is beginning to rival that of Mahan. See his *Towards an American Army: Military Thought from Washington to Marshall* (New York, Columbia University Press, 1962); *History of the United States Army* (New York, Macmillan, 1967); *The American Way of Warfare, A History of United States Military Strategy and Policy* (New York, Macmillan, 1973).
9. A good example of this is J.J. Johnson (ed.), *The Role of the Military in Underdeveloped Countries* (Princeton, Princeton University Press, 1962). See also H. Daalder, *The Role of the Military in the Emerging Countries* (The Hague, Mouton, 1962), and the articles in J. Van Doorn (ed.), *Armed Forces and Society* (The Hague, Mouton, 1968); *Military Profession and Military Regimes* (The Hague, Mouton, 1969).
10. See especially Aristide Zolberg, 'The Military Decade in Africa', *World Politics*, XXV, January 1973, pp. 309-31; R.M. Price, 'A Theoretical Theoretical Approach to Military Rule in New States', ibid., XXIII,

'A Theoretical Approach to Military Rule in New States', ibid., XXIII, April 1971, pp. 400-30; Amos Perlmutter, 'The Arab Military Elite', ibid., pp. 269-300.

11. See for instance, Harry L. Coles and A.K. Weinberg, *Civil Affairs: Soldiers Become Governors* (United States Army in World War II: Special Studies, Washington, Department of Army, 1964); C.J. Friedrich, *American Experiences in Military Government in World War II* (New York, Rinehart, 1948); J.D. Montgomery, *Forced to be Free: The Artificial Revolutions in Germany and Japan* (Chicago, University of Chicago Press, 1957). The British official account is to be found in F.V. Donnison, *Civil Affairs and Military Government: North-West Europe, 1944-6* (History of the Second World War, United Kingdom Military Series, London, HMSO, 1961).

12. See Chapter 15, 'Morality in Force in International Politics', in his *Studies in War and Peace* (London, Temple Smith, 1970), p. 239.

13. For a brief but elegant treatment of 'Wellington and the British Army', see M. Howard (ed.), *Wellingtonian Studies* (Aldershot, Gale and Polden, 1959), reprinted in *Studies in War and Peace*, pp. 50-64.

14. The most succinct study of this problem is by Marcus Cunliffe in his opening article, 'George Washington's Generalship', in G. Billias (ed.), *George Washington's Generals* (New York, Morrow, 1964), pp. 3-21. See also Weigley, *History of US Army*, pp. 67-73.

15. Weigley, ibid., p. 87.

16. Huntington, op. cit., pp. 157-63, 184-6

17. Ibid., p. 161.

18. Michael Howard, 'Military Science in an Age of Peace', *Royal United Service Institute Journal of Defence Studies*, CXIX, March 1974, pp. 3-10.

19. Sir Llewellyn Woodward, 'The Rise of the Professional Historian in England', K. Bourne and D.C. Watt (eds.), *Studies in International History* (London, Longmans, 1967), pp. 16-34.

20. One has in mind here the works of Colonel G.F.R. Henderson, Colonel C. Dalton and Sir John Fortescue. Wolseley was once asked to write a history of the American Civil War but, although he was a great admirer of Robert E. Lee, he did not do so.

21. Martin Kitchen, *The German Officer Corps, 1870-1914* (Oxford, Clarendon, 1967); *A Military History of Germany* (London, Weidenfeld and Nicolson, 1975).

22. Alfred Vagts, *A History of Militarism* (Greenwich, Meridian, 1959), pp. 312-18; Guy Chapman, 'The French Army in Politics', in Howard (ed.), *Soldiers and Governments*, pp. 51-72; G.A. Kelly, 'The French Army Re-enters Politics, 1940-55', *Political Science Quarterly*, LXXVI, 1961, pp. 367-92; P.M. de la Gorce, *The French Army: A Military-Political History* (London, Weidenfeld and Nicolson, 1963); D.B. Ralston, 'From Boulanger to Pétain: the Third Republic and the Republican Generals', B. Bond and I. Roy

(eds.), *War and Society* (London, Croom Helm, 1975).
23. Adrian Preston (ed.), *In Relief of Gordon* (London, Hutchinson, 1967); *The South African Diaries of Sir Garnet Wolseley, 1875* (Cape Town, Balkema, 1971); *The South African Journals of Sir Garnet Wolseley, 1879-80* (Cape Town, Balkema, 1973).
24. Leon Edel, *Henry James, 1870-81: The Conquest of London* (New York, Lippincott, 1962), p. 334.
25. Preston, op. cit., especially the Introduction.
26. Ibid.
27. Vagts, op. cit., p. 313.
28. D.W.R. Bahlman (ed.), *The Diary of Sir Edward Walter Hamilton, 1880-1885* (Oxford, Clarendon, 1972), I, p. 314.
29. A.B. Cooke and John Vincent, *The Governing Passion: Cabinet Government and Party Politics in Britain, 1885-86* (Brighton, Harvester Press, 1974).
30. Surprisingly, Sir Henry Wilson had the same idea. C.E. Callwell, *Field Marshal Sir Henry Wilson: His Life and Diaries* (London, Cassell, 1928), I, p.47.
31. John Gooch, 'Attitudes towards War in Late Victorian and Edwardian England', *War and Society*, 1975.
32. Adam Yarmolinsky, *The Military Establishment: Its Impact on American Society* (New York, Harper and Row, 1971).
33. Connell, *Wavell*, pp. 241-2.
34. Penderel Moon (ed.), *Wavell: The Viceroy's Journal* (London, Oxford University Press, 1973).
35. Charles de Gaulle, *The Edge of the Sword* (New York, Criterion, 1980); David Dilks (ed.), *The Diaries of Sir Alexander Cadogan, 1938-45* (New York, Pulman's, 1972), pp. 529, 533-4.
36. J.W.D. Trythall, *Franco: A Biography* (London, Hart Davis, 1970), p. 24; Crozier, *Franco*, pp. 29-32.
37. Stanley Hoffman, 'De Gaulle's Memoirs: The Hero as History', *World Politics*, XX, 1968, pp. 140-55; Douglas Johnson, 'The Political Principles of General De Gaulle', *International Affairs*, vol. 37, January 1961, pp. 650-62; Robert Aron, 'The Political Methods of General De Gaulle', ibid., pp. 19-28.
38. Wavell, *Allenby in Egypt* (London, Cassell, 1943).
39. Trythall, op. cit., pp. 59, 61-6.
40. E.K.G. Sixsmith, *Eisenhower as Military Commander* (New York, Stein and Day, 1973); Stephen Ambrose, *The Supreme Commander* (London, Cassell, 1971); A. Chandler and S. Ambrose (eds.), *The Papers of Dwight D. Eisenhower; the War Years* (Baltimore, Johns Hopkins Press, 1970).
41. Cunliffe in Billias (ed.), *Washington's Generals*, pp. 3-17.
42. Ibid., p. 16.
43. Ibid., p. 4.
44. Connell, *Wavell*, p. 47.
45. G. Mallaby, *From My Level: Unwritten Minutes* (London, Hutchinson, 1965), pp. 95-6.
46. Yarmolinsky, op. cit., p. 30.
47. Hoffman, op. cit., p. 148; Johnson, op. cit., p. 659.

48. Kinross, op. cit., pp. 467-8.
49. Moon, op. cit., p. 45.
50. Perlmutter, op., pp. 269-300; E. Beeri, *Army Officers in Arab Politics and Society* (London, Pall Mall Press, 1970).
51. A.P. Wavell, 'The Higher Commander', *Journal of the Royal United Service Institute*, LXXXI, February 1936, pp. 15-32; *Soldiers and Soldiering* (London, Cape, 1953); *The Palestine Campaigns* (London, Constable, 1931).
52. Sir Harold Nicolson, 'Wellington: The Diplomatist', in Howard (ed.), *Wellingtonian Studies*, pp. 41-56.
53. For the following see Moon's introduction and epilogue to Wavell's journal.
54. Peter Mansfield, *The British in Egypt* (New York, Holt, Rinehart and Winston, 1972), p. 227.
55. Moon, op. cit., pp. 3-4, 12, 23-4.
56. M.C. Brock, 'Wellington: The Statesman', in Howard (ed.), *Wellingtonian Studies*, pp. 57-76; C.R.M.F. Cruttwell, *Wellington* (London, Duckworth, 1936); J.R.M. Butler, *The Passing of the Great Reform Bill* (London, Longmans, 1914).
57. Mallaby, op. cit., p. 105.
58. Johnson, op. cit., p. 652.

Hindenburg

MARTIN KITCHEN

When Paul von Beneckendorf und von Hindenburg retired as the commanding general of IV Army Corps in 1911 at the age of sixty-four it seemed that a successful but unspectacular career had come to an end and that he could now enjoy a life of relative obscurity as a retired general in Hanover. Hindenburg was a man who was completely unknown to the vast majority of Germans. He was without influential friends, and having dared to criticise the Kaiser in the Imperial Manoeuvres in 1908 he was somewhat out of favour at court. His Army colleagues respected him, and the great Schlieffen had spoken highly of him, but all agreed that he had risen as high as his talents would merit and no one expected to hear anything more of this retired general, *à la suite* to the *Dritte Garde Regiment zu Fuss*.

On 22 August 1914 Hindenburg received a telegram from the Kaiser asking him to accept the command of the Eighth Army in East Prussia. Bored with his life in retirement and anxious to play his part in the war, he accepted eagerly. A new career was to begin which was to take him to unexpected heights. From the obscurity of retirement he was rapidly to become an almost mythical figure, a signifier of the hopes and aspirations of millions of Germans, the inspiration for heroic sacrifice, the guarantor of victory.

His appointment had little to do with his own abilities as an army commander. The failure of Prittwitz and his chief of staff, Waldersee, against the Russians in East Prussia had caused something of a panic, and the influential East Prussian landowners demanded action so that the Russian invader might be driven from their estates. There was agreement at Headquarters that the brilliant, outspoken and unpredictable Ludendorff should be sent to East Prussia as chief of staff, but who should be his superior officer? After some discussion the suggestion of Colonel von Fabeck, who knew Hindenburg well, was accepted. It was agreed that Hindenburg, although lacking any outstanding ability or qualities of military intellect, was known to be absolutely reliable, competent and with steady nerves, and as such would be an admirable restraining influence on Ludendorff, the two men complementing and strengthening one another.

Hindenburg's appointment was thus due more to Ludendorff's abilities than his own, and similarly, although the victory at Tannenberg was largely the work of Hoffmann and Ludendorff, it was Hindenburg who became a national hero; and owing to the successful efforts of his subordinates, the most successful army commander in the German Army. In a massive propaganda campaign designed to support flagging morale and to undermine the enemy's determination to fight, Hindenburg was made out to be the saviour of East Prussia, the guardian of German civilisation against the slavonic hordes. Photographs of his massive square head were hung in every patriotic home. Overnight he became the most popular and the most respected man in Germany.

Although the spectacular success of Tannenberg was not repeated, and although the battle was far from decisive, the reputations of Hindenburg and Ludendorff were undiminished in the following two years. They were to have further successes, but on their own these would not have been enough to keep the legend alive. It was the contrast with the failures and frustrations on the western front that made them seem so much larger than life. Once again it was the limitations of others which made Hindenburg appear in such a favourable light rather than his own achievements and abilities.

With the Schlieffen plan in ruins after the defeat on the Marne, and the failure to outflank the *Entente* during the 'race for the sea' in September 1914, two lines of trenches stretched from the Channel to the Swiss border. The new chief of the German General Staff, Falkenhayn, tried to punch a hole through the *Entente's* lines near Ypres in the hope of being able to roll back the front. The result was a costly failure which showed up the great superiority of the defence in trench warfare and the frightening losses which any offensive was likely to incur. Falkenhayn concluded that Schlieffen's plan for a massive war of annihilation would have to be abandoned in favour of a war of attrition based on a series of limited operations which would avoid the terrible losses of the two battles of Ypres, but which would gradually wear down the resistance of the *Entente*.

Falkenhayn's strategy of attrition, although ingenious, overlooked the unfortunate fact that with its virtually limitless reserves of men and materials the *Entente* was almost bound to win a prolonged slogging match, however unimaginative its generals might be. He thus tried to find an alternative strategy which would combine elements of the annihilation and the attrition strategies. This new strategy was put to the test in the attack on Verdun in 1916. The idea was not to take the fortress at Verdun but rather to threaten it constantly with a series of limited operational attacks which would draw more and more Frenchmen into a trap where they could be destroyed by massive artillery bombardments. The plan was imaginative, but it underestimated the resilience of the *Entente* and the losses that could be inflicted even in limited attacks. Even more serious were the ambiguities in the plan which led local commanders to attempt to take the fortresses, rather than menacing them, so that the Verdun offensive soon degenerated into another Ypres, and was a costly failure. Kitchener's army on the Somme proved far more effective than Falkenhayn had hoped. In the east the Brussilov offensive threatened to destroy the Austrian Army which had also lost Görz to the Italians. In August 1916 Rumania declared war on the Central Powers. Falkenhayn's gamble had failed. There was now virtual unanimity that since Moltke and Falkenhayn had both failed to bring victory, the victor of Tannenberg who had turned the setback in the east into a cool and decisive victory, a classic battle of encirclement which had earned him the title of the new Hannibal, should replace him at the high command. Hindenburg had no sympathy for Falkenhayn's strategy of attrition, and insisted that if only the chief of general staff would give him the men and materials he could win a decisive campaign of annihilation in the east which would free the troops there for the final battle in the west which would settle the war. This was an attractive prospect which seemed to be the only possible way that Germany could win the decisive victory which she felt she needed. There was no serious debate on these strategic alternatives. Falkenhayn was the man of Verdun, Hindenburg of Tannenberg, and only a new Tannenberg could secure Germany as a world power and enable her to achieve her ambitious war aims.

But although Hindenburg's appointment was seen as the most promising way out of the deadlock on the western front, there were other equally important factors which led to the change in the High Command in August 1916. Schlieffen's plan for a swift campaign was designed to avoid the problems of a long and protracted war which would place an intolerable strain on the German economy. As the war had become a war of attrition problems of war production became increasingly important. Up until the summer of 1916 there had only been modest attempts to control the economy by channelling supplies of raw materials, foodstuffs and manpower to an extent sufficient to ensure an adequate production of necessary war materials. As the 'battle of materials' began to dominate the war the demands on industry became increasingly pressing, the economic superiority of the *Entente* became ever more apparent, and there were insistent demands for a total mobilisation and regimentation of the economy to meet this critical situation. As early as 1915 industrialists like Hugo Stinnes began discussions with Hindenburg and Ludendorff, pushing for controls which would favour heavy industry. At the High Command Colonel Bauer, an expert on heavy artillery and an outspoken critic of Falkenhayn, forged close links with the leaders of heavy industry, and agreement was reached that the existing bureaucracy under the War Ministry was cumbersome and inefficient, that the War Ministry was far too conciliatory towards labour, and that suggestions that there should be controls on excessive war profits and on the still flourishing export trade were creating an unhealthy atmosphere and a loss of confidence. On 23 August 1916 the *Verein Deutscher Eisenhüttenleute*, a powerful organisation of heavy industry, sent a memorandum to the Government and to Hindenburg arguing that an increase in production was only possible if there was a drastic reorganisation of the War Ministry and its procurement agencies, and if this did not take place Germany's prospects looked exceedingly grim.

The industrialists who pressed for Hindenburg's appointment were hoping for a radical change. They wanted the regimentation of labour so that output and profits could be maximised, they hoped for a significant structural change within German industry which would further enhance the position of heavy industry, and they called for the ruthless exploitation of the occupied territories for men and materials. August 1916 was thus celebrated as a triumph for heavy industry.

Two years of war had also placed an extraordinary strain on a social system which was seriously outmoded and which was no longer adequate for the exigencies of a modern industrial society. The War Ministry and most senior government officials were prepared to support Bethmann Hollweg's broadly conciliatory policy, and accepted the idea of consultation with the unions and limited internal reforms, but there were those who felt that such a policy would only serve to encourage further and more radical demands. Such men argued that massive war aims would be sufficient recompense for the present misery, and that the prospect of vast gains in the future would prepare the people to accept even greater sacrifices. They hoped that Hindenburg would put a stop to Bethmann Hollweg's weak-kneed policy and also engineer the victory which would enable the achievement of their wild territorial ambitions.

As this military, economic and social crisis developed the structural weaknesses of the Reich Government became increasingly apparent. The constitution did not provide institutional means of integration, for its bias was both conservative and anti-parliamentary. Integration had to be provided by a figure who could inspire general approval and acclamation. This meant that there was a bonapartist moment within the system, and William II's brand of charismatic leadership and popular absolutism which he practised at the beginning of his reign was a perfectly adequate interpretation of his constitutional function. But during the war the Kaiser relinquished much of his authority, for all the glamour of his title of 'Supreme Warlord', and as a result of his reluctance to overcome the differences between the civilian and military leadership they became more severe. The inevitable result was a further strengthening of the power of the High Command. The military dismissed all criticisms as unwarranted interference by 'idiotic civilians' and 'inkpot diplomats' in purely technical matters on which they were not competent to voice an opinion. Those in the Army who wished to see Falkenhayn dismissed and replaced by Hindenburg hoped that the new head of the High Command would further strengthen the hand of the Army over the civilians and also provide the figurehead whose commanding presence would restore the unity and sense of purpose which the badly tattered political truce of 1914, the *Burgfrieden,* was no longer able to do. Hindenburg's role as *ersatz* Kaiser in this sense dates back to 1916, and was not merely the result of the problems of the Weimar Republic.

The appointment of Hindenburg to the High Command in 1916 was thus the result of a five-fold crisis. It was hoped that he would find a solution to the military situation which Falkenhayn had failed to master. Heavy industry hoped that he would control and regiment the economy to their advantage, and put an end to the War Ministry's unpopular economic policies. It was hoped that a popular and respected figure like Hindenburg would help to contain the social crisis and end what his supporters felt to be a misguided policy of conciliation of labour. It was also hoped that he would end the squabbles between the military and the civilians and unite the country in a common effort. Lastly, his supporters hoped that he would bring victory, not merely the defeat of the *Entente* but the massive war aims which alone would secure Germany's position as a world power and justify the sacrifices demanded of the German people. The intrigue against Falkenhayn was successful. The politicians, crowned heads, government departments, military leaders and industrialists were jubilant at their success. It was hoped that Hindenburg would electrify the nation and make the war popular once again, even with the dissident social democrats. The vast majority of Germans imagined that the multiple crisis which had affected all levels of society would now be solved and that the war would take an immediate and dramatic turn for the better.

It soon became clear, however, that whereas it had been simple to criticise Falkenhayn from the security of High Command East, Hindenburg was soon obliged to admit that his predecessor's objections to a more extensive campaign in the east were substantially correct. Troops simply could not be spared from the western front without running the severe risk of a breakthrough by the forces of the *Entente*. At the same time Russia had to be defeated if the east were to be reorganised under German hegemony. Without such a victory in the east Germany would be unable to devote all her efforts to the final struggle in the west. Thus Hindenburg was forced by the harsh realities of the military situation to adopt Falkenhayn's over-all strategy, which he had so bitterly criticised before his appointment to the High Command. It was not until the February Revolution in Russia that any significant change was possible. Troops were immediately sent from the east to the west, but when it became clear that the Lvov-Miliukov Government was determined to continue the war, Hindenburg found himself in the rather peculiar situation of supporting a social revolution in Russia which would destroy the bourgeois liberal government's ability to continue the war. The intoxicating vision of an annexationist peace in Russia blinded Hindenburg to the dangers to autocratic Germany of a revolutionary regime in Russia.

But Hindenburg had not been appointed to the High Command simply to maintain the *status quo*. By November 1916 he had been forced to admit that unless there were some significant change in the overall situation there could be no question of another Tannenberg and that the war was indeed one of attrition. The only way out of this impasse seemed to him to be unrestricted submarine warfare, which it was hoped would bring England to her knees before America or any of the other neutral states could intervene. When German troops entered Bucharest on 6 December 1916 Hindenburg agreed to the immediate commencement of unrestricted submarine warfare, arguing that the situation in the land war was now sufficiently stable that there was no immediate danger of an attack from Holland or Denmark. At the crown council meeting on 9 January 1917, Bethmann Hollweg was forced to abandon his impractical scheme for a 'third way' which would extend the submarine war without bringing America into the struggle, and the third great *va banque* play of the war began.

Like the Schlieffen plan and the Verdun offensive, unrestricted submarine warfare was also a failure. Within a few weeks it became all too obvious that the exaggerated hopes of the submarine enthusiasts were hopelessly unrealistic and the war continued as a bloody slogging match, the *Entente* gaining a valuable new ally in the United States. The realisation in August 1916 that Falkenhayn was substantially correct in seeing the war as a war of attrition was finally confirmed by the failure of the submarine campaign. As the strategy of annihilation was an objective impossibility Hindenburg was obliged to place greater emphasis on a marked increase in the production of war materials. Two days after his appointment Hindenburg outlined his ideas on stepping up war production in a memorandum to the War Minister. He demanded a threefold increase in the production of artillery and machine guns and a one hundred per cent increase in the production of ammunition by the spring. Women and children would have to be used as additional manpower so that the Army would not have to cut the size of its reserves. Heavy industry should be particularly favoured, and small firms producing non-essential goods should be allowed to go to the wall. Hindenburg and his supporters in heavy industry wanted the regimentation and militarisation of industry, an acceleration of the tendency towards centralisation and monopolisation, substantial interference with the free workings of the economy and a maximisation of war output.

The goals of this 'Hindenburg programme' were hopelessly unrealistic and the proposed method of attaining them was opposed by the Chancellor, the War Minister and most of the civilian government who argued that cooperation between capital and labour was by far the most efficient way of increasing output and that massive state intervention in the workings of the economy would be seriously disruptive. A compromise was therefore reached in which a War Office (*Kriegsamt*) was created under the able leadership of General Groener, with responsibilities for procurement and allocation of raw materials, the production of guns and ammunition, fuel, and the control of labour resources. Nominally under the War Ministry, the *Kriegsamt* had to endure the constant interference and cajoling of the High Command. Its field of competence was ill-defined, its bureaucracy cumbersome and top-heavy. As the antagonisms between the High Command and the civilians became more acute there was little room for the sort of compromise on which the *Kriegsamt* was based.

In December 1916 the Auxiliary Labour Law (*Hilfsdienstgesetz*) was passed by the Reichstag at the insistence of the High Command. The Bill was a somewhat

amended version of the original drastic proposals submitted by
Hindenburg. All male Germans between the ages of seventeen
and sixty were required to perform essential war duties, but as
there was no attempt made to define what kind of work was
deemed essential, the law was only applied to the working class
and to some less-favoured white-collar workers. Workers were
now unable to leave a place of employment without permission,
but they were given permission if they could show that an
improvement of working conditions would result from the
proposed move. In practice this meant that workers were free to
enter the armaments industries because wages were high, and
heavy industry was guaranteed an adequate supply of labour
under the terms of the Act. Fines and even prison sentences
could be given to workers who refused offers of employment.
But the most controversial provision in the Bill was for the
establishment of workers' councils, institutions which were
celebrated by the moderate left as 'war socialism' and
bemoaned by the right as a major step towards Communism. In
fact the councils had little power and were designed as a means
of letting off steam rather than as a significant step towards
industrial democracy.

The Hindenburg Programme and the Auxiliary Labour Law
were not sufficient to overcome Germany's economic problems.
Legislation and coercion could not overcome the fact that there
was a serious shortage of essentials such as coal and
transportation. But Hindenburg and his staff refused to accept
this simple fact, and demanded draconic measures to force
higher output. Within a remarkably short space of time
Hindenburg blamed his own Bill, or more precisely the
amended version as adopted by the Reichstag, for all
Germany's shortcomings on the home front, including rising
wages in some sectors, inflation, swollen profits, industrial
unrest and shortages of raw materials and food. Groener, who
had urged a degree of cooperation between capital and labour,
and who had been murmuring about curbing profit margins,
lost his job at the *Kriegsamt* in August 1917, having fallen foul
of Hindenburg and Ludendorff.

Frustration with the failure of the Auxiliary Labour Law led
Hindenburg to demand the use of emergency powers to
regiment labour, but he was unable to find enough support from
the civilian authorities for such a drastic step. Then he tried to

be more conciliatory and pursued a policy which was very similar to that of Groener, but with the January strikes of 1918 he reverted to his old intransigent attitude. Unable to find any solution to the economic problems of the country Hindenburg began to blame the home front for attacking the Army from the rear. Thus the failure of his economic policy provided rich material for the 'stab in the back' legend which was to play such a powerful ideological role in the Weimar Republic.

The failure of the High Command's economic policies further intensified the social tensions which Hindenburg's appointment had been designed to assuage. For the majority of Germans the war meant deprivation and even ruin, whereas a small minority profited immensely from the sharply rising prices and shortages. Unable to find a military solution to the war, and with the failure of the economic policies of the Army, the High Command fell back on propaganda and calls for further sacrifices. Prompted by the ever active and extremist Colonel Bauer, Hindenburg made a number of pronouncements on domestic politics which are highly indicative of the ideological stance of the Army leadership. He believed that compulsion could solve many of Germany's problems. The idle could be forced to do an honest day's work, speculators could be obliged to make their contribution to the war effort. He made rousing appeals for the end of party factionalism and to all absurd notions of the equality of man. But at the same time he felt that this stern medicine would have to be sweetened by vague ideas about improvements of the social services, particularly for war veterans, and an extensive land settlement programme, mainly in the east. Hindenburg also knew that sacrifices could not be reasonably demanded of the people unless some attempt was made to curb excessive profits and wild speculation. He shared the irrational anti-capitalism of many officers which opposed capitalism for destroying social stability, ruining the middle class, reducing humanity to mere cogs in the machinery of profit and spawning a vicious and virulent socialism which seemed to threaten the very foundations of society. Yet this did not deter him from continuing to give his full support to heavy industry and thus intensifying the conditions which be bemoaned. Unable to find any way out of this logical impasse he resorted to wild accusations against the political leadership for creating social divisions by their feeble-mindedness, against the materialism and greed of the masses, and against the treasonable activities of the trade unions and socialists. The only bribe that Hindenburg could offer was the 'Hindenburg Victory' which would bring massive annexations, but the contradiction between these excessive aims and the military and economic means of attaining them served further to intensify the crisis. The social question could not be even partially solved without the High Command accepting the idea of peace without annexations and contributions, but this Hindenburg would not, and could not, accept.

Such pronouncements on social policy showed that Bethmann Hollweg's hopes that the appointment of Hindenburg to the High Command would end the rivalry between the High Command and the civilians were seriously misplaced. Hindenburg knew full well that public opinion had played an important part in his appointment which seemed to be as much the result of a form of presidential election as it was of the exercise of the Kaiser's power of command. He soon came to believe that in some mysterious way he embodied the general will of the German people, and thus stood outside the constitution and its restraints. This pseudo-democratic dimension to the politics of the High Command was something quite new in the history of German militarism. The Army was beginning to shed its aloofness and arrogant isolation and indulge in a bonapartist rabble-rousing which would have been profoundly shocking to earlier generations. The Kaiser was fully aware of the implications of this tendency, and for this reason initially resisted Hindenburg's appointment to the High Command, fearing that to give way to the pressure of public opinion would be to introduce a dangerously democratic precedent into constitutional practice.

There were those, chief among them Colonel Bauer, who argued that Hindenburg should exploit this situation to establish a direct military dictatorship. Hindenburg would not accept this suggestion. For him it was too radical a break with the traditional role of the Army which always pretended to be politically neutral; it was also too abrupt a departure from the bonapartist traditions of Bismarck's authoritarian régime, and it did not suit Hindenburg's character, for he always preferred to remain behind the scenes so that he might appear to transcend the bitter daily struggles of the politicians. In

Ludendorff's phrase, it was better to use the civilian government as a lightning conductor so that it could bear the blame for the failures of the High Command's policies. Hindenburg was thus able to secure the dismissal of Bethmann Hollweg, the War Minister, Wild, the chief of the civil cabinet, Valentini, the State Secretary, Kühlmann, the chief of the naval staff, Holtzendorff, and other lesser dignitaries. By sending off these political scapegoats into the wilderness Hindenburg was able to strengthen his own power. Thus, paradoxically, the more the High Command hid behind the civilian government, and the more they claimed to be solely concerned with military affairs, the greater was their political power and influence.

Although Hindenburg rejected the idea of a military dictatorship he was even more outspoken in his criticisms of all who suggested that certain political concessions were needed to lessen domestic political tensions. After a long and bitter struggle, he managed to postpone any further discussions of the long overdue reform of the Prussian franchise, which had been outlined in the Kaiser's message to the German nation at Easter 1917. In the place of reform Hindenburg demanded authority and discipline and the bold affirmation of such irrational concepts as race, leadership, the national interest and the *Volksgemeinschaft*.

Excessive war aims were regarded as the most suitable panacea for the problems facing German society. Hindenburg argued that these war aims were a strategic necessity, and as such were a 'purely military' concern. Germany was surrounded by powerful enemies who were bent on revenge after their defeat by the central powers; therefore vast annexations were needed to make Germany an impregnable fortress against any conceivable attack. Thus, by a perverse logic, the more desperate Germany's military situation became, the more excessive were the demands for war aims. Germany's weakness was taken as proof that even greater guarantees of security were needed in the future. Germany needed to be autarchic, in order to be able to fight the final battle for world domination. Hindenburg's thinking on war aims thus combined a social-imperialist moment with promises of annexations dangling like a succulent carrot in front of the noses of a suffering population, with an ominous prefiguration of Nazi ambitions. The product of strife, bitterness and weakness, the national dream was sour and excessive.

Hindenburg was able to secure the adoption of most of his war aims. His persistent demands for the domination of Belgium made any peace initiative with the *Entente* impossible. The failure of his scheme to create an 'independent' Poland so as to form an allied Polish Army was blamed on the civilians. As relations with Austria-Hungary grew steadily worse, Hindenburg demanded a 'purely military' solution — *Anschluss* with Germany, by force if necessary, and the creation of a new set of client states in the Balkans. In his eastern policy he incorporated two powerful motivating forces of German policy: imperialist ambitions towards the east, and anti-Bolshevism, the new and intensified form of the anti-Russian dimension of Bismarck's bonapartism. This policy was to reach a climax during the negotiations over the treaty of Brest-Litovsk, when his tactics of threatened resignation, 'purely military' arguments, and extremist demands were used to the full. In spite of the objections of the Foreign Office, the High Command pursued a relentless policy of conquest in the east, even though the situation on the western front was growing increasingly critical. German troops occupied the Baltic states, and marched into Rumania, the Caucasus, the Crimea and the Black Sea coast, the Trans-Caucasus and the Caspian, and also mounted an expedition to Finland.

Hindenburg was unable to win a military victory, and was thus unable to solve the five-fold crisis which he had been called upon to master. Only a massive victory would have compensated for the suffering of the mass of Germans, but this was militarily and economically impossible. By August 1918 Hindenburg no longer looked invincible, indeed the demi-gods at the High Command began to appear woefully mortal. The Reichstag was able to strengthen its hand against the Army, but this did not mean any significant strengthening of parliamentary institutions in Germany, for the politicians were hopelessly compromised. They were forced into the position of having to accept responsibility for the consequences of defeat. The 'lightning conductor' policy scored another major success. The prestige of the Army, and particularly of Hindenburg, remained intact.

On 10 November 1918 Hindenburg announced that he would support the social democratic régime of Ebert in order to 'stop the spread of terroristic Bolshevism in Germany'. At the beginning of December Army units in Berlin attempted a counter-revolutionary *coup*. Although it was a failure, owing to the determined resistance of the Berlin workers, Hindenburg immediately presented Ebert with a list of political demands which included the cancellation of the powers of the workers' and soldiers' councils, the abolition of councils in the Army and a reaffirmation of the officers' power of command. Ebert preferred to bide his time, but he allowed General Lequis to move his troops into Berlin, greeting them at the Brandenburg Gate with the words 'We welcome you back home with joyful hearts, the enemy did not defeat you!' The social democrat Ebert thus accepted Hindenburg's contention that the Army had been 'stabbed in the back'.

A further threat to the Army was the 'Hamburg Points' passed by the Congress of Worker' and Soldiers' Councils on 18 December 1918. Hindenburg promptly threatened to resign if Ebert accepted the Hamburg Points, and in return for a rather lame assurance that the Army was not thinking of engineering a counter-revolution, the Council of Peoples' Representatives agreed to ignore the points. Secure in the knowledge that the old Army would survive after the upheavals of defeat and revolution, Hindenburg could now afford to retire. On 3 July 1919 he left his headquarters at Coberg, bitterly denouncing the Carthaginian peace of Versailles. He returned to Hanover, where he was welcomed like a hero, and began work dictating his dull and uncommunicative memoirs.

It was not long before attempts were made to bring him back into political life. Colonel Bauer had lost none of his appetite for political intrigue and as a determined enemy of the new republic he hoped to persuade Hindenburg to stand for election to the Presidency in 1919 as the candidate of the 'national' factions. He hoped that Hindenburg would use the office of President to establish some form of dictatorship, but Hindenburg was as reluctant as ever to come out into the open and resisted Bauer's suggestions. The the Kaiser let Hindenburg know that he favoured his candidature, and it would seen that Hindenburg would have consented to stand had the Kapp *putsch* not intervened, the failure of which discredited the right-wing parties and Bauer, who played an important role in the *coup*, fled the country. Hindenburg did not approve of the Kapp *putsch*, largely because it was mis-managed, but he flatly refused to speak out publicly against it, thus letting it be known that he sympathised with the enemies of the republic.

His essential hostility towards the new régime was given wider publicity when he appeared before the parliamentary commission whose task was to examine the causes of Germany's defeat. He insisted that the Army had indeed been 'stabbed in the back', and by doing so he branded the democratic politicians as traitors and gave considerable aid to the right-wing enemies of the republic. His attitude towards the republic can also be clearly seen in a letter he wrote to his old companion-in-arms, Ludendorff, after the abortive 'Hitler *putsch*' in Munich in 1923. He did not condemn the *putsch* attempt out of hand, any more than he had done the Kapp *putsch*. He argued that Hitler's great fault had been to be too impulsive, and he was annoyed that Ludendorff had allowed himself to become involved in an escapade which had served to discredit the right and which had associated sections of the Army too closely with extremist politics.

Ebert's sudden death in 1925 precipitated a Presidential election for which the anti-republican parties were ill-prepared. There seemed to be no way of stopping the republican candidate, Marx. The obvious candidates, like Seeckt, Krupp or a Hohenzollern, were altogether too obvious and represented sectional interests. Hindenburg seemed to be the one man who transcended party factionalism and seemed to symbolise the unity of the fatherland, the greatness of imperial Germany, an omen of better times ahead. But not everyone on the right agreed. There were those who felt that he had compromised with the republic by refusing to condemn it openly and outspokenly. Revisionists like Stresemann thought that his election would compromise negotiations with the victorious powers, for Hindenburg's uncompromising attitude towards the peace treaty was well known. Moderate republicans like Delbrück hoped that Hindenburg would help to reconcile the right with the republic, and that the ranks would close behind a genuine national figure. The main problem for the Hindenburg supporters was to get the old man to accept the nomination and to come out into the open to play a direct political role. At first Hindenburg refused to enter what was to him the sordid turmoil of a Presidential election. It was Admiral Tirpitz who managed to persuade him that his candidature was apolitical, and that he would be standing for the unity of the country rather than for any particular faction.

Hindenburg made almost no effort to campaign, and hardly appeared in public, so as to underline the fact that he was not a 'political' candidate. Yet nothing was further from the truth. The sole reason for his candidature was to stop Marx, who seemed to be the almost invincible candidate of the republicans. A vote for Hindenburg was in most instances a vote against the republic, and at best an expression of toleration rather than support. The fact that he failed to get an absolute majority of votes made it even more difficult for him to claim to be a genuinely national choice. Indeed, this belief that he in some mysterious way embodied the aspirations of the nation was as illusory in 1925 as it had been in 1916. As the country was seriously divided his refusal to take sides simply made the situation worse, for he was denounced from all sides as a trimmer and certainly could not be seen as an integrator. To the disgust of the republicans he did nothing for the republic, but the extreme right was equally furious that he did nothing very much against it either.

From the outset of his Presidency he used his position as chairman of the Cabinet Council *(Kabinettsrat)* to deliver outspoken attacks on the Treaty of Versailles, the war guilt clause, the demilitarisation of the Rhineland, disarmament, the inter-allied military commission, the Poles and the territorial settlement in the East. But in the relatively prosperous and stable years from 1925 to 1929 Hindenburg was able to avoid any major political confrontations. His election acted as a restraining influence on the political ambitions of the Army, for whereas Seeckt had been able to dazzle Ebert with 'purely military' arguments in the style of the High Command during the war, he could not possibly do this to Hindenburg. Seeckt would hint that Ebert only ruled by gracious permission of the Army, but it was unthinkable that a mere general would dare to use this argument with the Field Marshal. Seeckt was obliged to discuss only military subjects with the new President, and complained bitterly that his political influence had been drastically reduced. In these early years the crisis over the German flag was probably the most important. Hindenburg would neither accept the traditional black, red and gold colours of the imperial flag, nor the exclusive use of the black, red and gold colours of the republic, and he hoped to find a way out of the dilemma by allowing both flags to be flown side by side at German missions outside Europe. Passions ran high, and Luther's Cabinet fell, but Hindenburg escaped without too much damage to his reputation, although the extreme right were strengthened in their conviction that he had sold out to the republic, the republicans that he was a determined opponent of the new regime.

With the beginnings of the crisis which was to lead to the destruction of the republic. Hindenburg began to play an increasingly active political role. When the Prussian Minister for the Interior, Grzesinski — a man who had incidentally welcomed Hindenburg to Kassel in 1918 on behalf of the social democratic movement, attempted to ban the *Stahlhelm* in the Rhineland and Westphalia where it had caused a number of provocative breaches of the peace, Hindenburg refused to agree, and the ban was lifted. But by accepting without any sign of enthusiasm the provisions of the Young Plan in the same year he was promptly denounced by the right for 'betraying the heroes of Langemarck', a bitter cut which hurt Hindenburg to the quick.

As the crisis deepened it became obvious that if the republic was to survive an alliance of all the republican parties was needed. Yet Hindenburg worked in the opposite direction, a policy that was bound to be a failure. Although he liked and supported Brüning, particularly in the early stages of his Chancellorship, he constantly urged him to open up his Cabinet to the right and to get rid of the more moderate members such as Groener, Stegerwald and Dietrich. He was unhappy at Groener's ban on the SS and SA, and wanted the ban to be extended to cover the paramilitary organisations of the social democratic and Communist parties. But this policy did nothing to gain support from his natural allies on the right. Field Marshal Mackensen refused to support Hindenburg in the 1932 Presidential elections on the grounds that he would not break completely with the social democrats, and voted instead for Hitler. By 1932 the Nazis were openly hostile to Hindenburg and speakers like Goebbels revelled in vituperative attacks on the old man. Hugenberg, another opponent from the right, ably supported by Hitler, managed to stop Brüning's plan to get Hindenburg's term of office extended by the Reichstag rather than have yet another election when it was obvious that he was unlikely to live for another full term. With such mounting hostility from the right it became almost impossible for Hindenburg to create a new government further to the right of Brüning's original Cabinet, for Hugenberg, who would have to be included in such a Cabinet, would not agree to the terms.

Whereas in 1925 Hindenburg had been dragged out of retirement to stop Marx and the republicans, in 1932 he was the candidate of those who opposed Hitler and who wanted to save the republic, either out of genuine democratic conviction or because the prospect of a Fascist regime in Germany was intolerable. There could now be no question of Hindenburg standing as a national candidate, and his failure to unite the nation made it only a matter of time before an arrangement would be made between the extreme right-wing parties which would mark a significant change in the political course of the republic.

Unlike 1925 Hindenburg won a clear majority of 53 per cent of the total number of votes cast. This was convincing proof that a wide selection of political points of view could combine in an attempt to save the republic from the extreme right, but Hindenburg ignored his democratic mandate and continued on his misguided and dangerous course. After the election Brüning suggested severing all ties with the social democrats, such as they were, and steering a nationalist course. But Brüning had little time to test this scheme, for Hindenburg objected to the Chancellor's proposal for selling off the bankrupt estates of the Junkers and accused the Chancellor of 'agrarian bolshevism' — a term that enjoyed wide currency in extreme right-wing circles. Brüning was refused the emergency powers which he requested, and was thus forced to resign.

Largely on the advice of Schleicher, who from 1930 had a decisive influence on Hindenburg's political thinking, Hindenburg appointed von Papen Chancellor in the hopes of creating a 'national' government. The idea behind the appointment was to take the wind out of Hitler's sails by a move to the right in the hope of not losing the support of those who had voted for Hindenburg on the grounds that almost anything was better than Hitler. This was not only a betrayal of the mandate of the 1932 election, it was political folly of the most extraordinary order. Papen was a suave and urbane aristocrat but he was a political moron, his career a succession of disasters of such spectacular stupidity as to border on the humorous. To Papen's credit he first refused Hindenburg's offer, but then as a mere lieutenant-colonel he submitted to the command of his superior officer. That a man like Papen could take any support away from Hitler was a derisory idea. When it came to playing the game of right-wing politics none could match the leader of the NSDAP.

When it became evident that the Papen experiment was a miserable failure, Schleicher told Hindenburg that a civil war was imminent which the Reichswehr would be unable to control and that it was time for Schleicher himself to attempt to form a government. Hindenburg at first resented this move as political meddling by the Army which amounted to disobedience to the President. Finally he parted from Papen, muttering that he was too old for a civil war, and giving him an autographed portrait with the words of the old army song *'ich hatt' einen Kameraden'* inscribed upon it. Hindenburg was very reluctant to appoint Schleicher, for he was becoming increasingly irritated by his constant scheming and plotting and he still could not reconcile himself to the idea of a soldier as Chancellor. He soon had occasion to regret the appointment, for Schleicher demanded powers to dismiss the Reichstag and ban both the Nazi and the Communist parties, having failed in his efforts to split the Nazi Party and form a coalition between the 'left-wing' Nazis and the trade unionists. Hindenburg refused, saying that Schleicher had been appointed in order to avoid a civil war, not to precipitate one.

The failure of Schleicher's attempt to find some alternative to an ultra-right government made Hitler's appointment a certainty. Hammerstein warned Hindenburg that there were only two alternatives open to him: either to appoint a second Papen Government, or a Hitler Cabinet. Little did he know that Papen had been busy negotiating with Hitler and had gained the support of influential industrialists for the Nazi Party. Even Schleicher now agreed that a Hitler Government was the only possible course of action, and he hoped to be appointed Reichswehr Minister in the new Cabinet. Hindenburg disliked Hitler, finding him coarse and vulgar. By referring to him as 'that Austrian corporal' he was expressing his dislike of Austria and his disdain for the other ranks. On the other hand Hitler, after an initial disastrous interview, soon learned how to charm the old man and treated him with almost servile respect. It was also obvious that a government with Hitler as Chancellor, Papen as Vice-Chancellor and with eight right-wingers who were not members of the Nazi Party, was as close as Hindenburg was likely to get to the 'national government' for which he had been striving since the fall of the Müller social democratic government in 1930.

There was widespread belief on the moderate right that the combination of Hindenburg and Hitler was as near to the ideal as possible. The hero of Tannenberg would hold the wild man from Bohemia in check, and Hitler would provide the dynamism and the idealism that had been lacking in German politics. Nothing could have been further from the truth. As Hitler's vicious régime went from excess to excess Hindenburg did nothing to restrain it. The respect shown to the old régime, in the person of Hindenburg, by the new order was an empty farce cynically stage-managed by Goebbels to placate the less radical nationalists. The empty chair left for the absent Emperor during the ceremonies at Potsdam to open the new Reichstag may have satisfied Hindenburg that he was indeed the trustee of the Emperor, but did he pause for a moment to think that he had betrayed the 19½ million voters who had given him their support in order to stop Hitler? It is doubtful if a man who had shown so little loyalty in the past to men like the Kaiser, Ludendorff, or Brüning was much troubled by such thoughts.

Hindenburg soon forgot whatever objections he might have had to Hitler. His birthday greetings to the *Führer* were unusually cordial, expressing his appreciation of his 'great patriotic work' and he closed with his 'comradely greetings'. Hindenburg had found a new *Kamarad*, but there was little time left to him to put his fidelity to the test.

The last major crisis Hindenburg had to face as President was the 'Röhm *putsch*' of 1934. He did nothing to protest against this criminal act in which the Reichswehr had played an important role. To Meissner, who ran the President's office, he remarked: 'For months I have told the Chancellor to get rid of this immoral and dangerous Röhm and lock him up; unfortunately he did not listen to me, and now it has again cost much blood.' Although his close associate, Schleicher, was brutally murdered he remained silent. His only concern was about the fate of Papen who had been arrested after a speech he made at Marburg in which he made a moderate conservative attack on the excesses of the new régime. Hindenburg ordered Blomberg to secure his release.

On 2 August 1934, only a few days after the Rohm affair, Hindenburg died. Hitler interrupted his visit to Bayreuth to visit the old man on his death-bed. Hindenburg regained consciousness as Hitler entered the room, and referred to the Chancellor as 'Your Majesty'. It was a tragi-comic end to a long career which had brought him fame, wealth and distinction but which from the heady days of August 1914 was a chain of failures, disappointments and betrayals. It was a bitter irony that the text he chose for his own funeral was: 'Be thou faithful unto death, and I will give thee a crown of life.' Certainly this is how Hindenburg would like to be remembered. A simple soldier who did his duty, who worked tirelessly for what he deemed to be the good of his beloved country and its monarchy. But history is neither so simple nor so forgiving.

How then can we assess Hindenburg, the soldier and the statesman? In the conventional sense he was undoubtedly a great man, the hero of a nation, field marshal and President. He ranks with figures like MacMahon, Horthy, Mannerheim and Pilsudski, but certainly not with Napoleon or even Wellington. But how much was there of true greatness behind the façade, what was the reality of the 'wooden titan'? As a soldier he was conscientious, devoted to duty and level-headed, but he lacked imagination, creativity and intelligence. During the war there were senior officers of greater military ability than Hindenburg in the German Army, among them Falkenhayn and Mackensen. His reputation as a soldier rested on a victory which was not his own, though it must be added that he enabled his subordinates to fight a successful battle and his cool nerve was a source of strength. But from being a reliable commanding officer, he became regarded as the only possible alternative to Falkenhayn, not so much because of his own qualities, but because Falkenhayn had failed. Then, as Germany's position became increasingly perilous, he seemed to be the only hope. He was called upon not only to win a military victory, but also to solve the economic, social, political and constitutional crises. Unable to solve the military problem he could not solve the others, and by pursuing extremist policies, both at home and abroad, while the military situation worsened, he further aggravated the situation. Yet Hindenburg was always able to shift the responsibility for his own failures on to others, insisting that his role was purely military and that he left politics to the politicians. In this manner the responsibility for defeat was placed on the democrats and the home front, and the myth of an undefeated Army was given his weighty support. No one did more to foster the idea of the 'stab in the back' than Hindenburg, and this obfuscation of the failures of the Army and the true position of Germany played an immensely harmful role in the history of the Weimar Republic.

As President he tried to continue this policy of the lightning conductor, but it could not work. He was unable to pretend to be a mere soldier, for he was at the very centre of politics. In the last years of his Presidency he was shown up to be a hollow man, refusing the support that was offered him, stubbornly following a course that was bound to lead to disaster. He offered no support to those who had voted for him in 1932, and the radical right despised him as a doddering old fool who had sold out to the republic. Ludendorff wrote to him immediately after he had appointed Hitler Chancellor: 'I solemnly prophesy to you that this damnable man will plunge our Reich into the abyss and bring inconceivable misery down upon our nation. Coming generations will curse you in your grave because of this action.' Historians have, on the whole, been more charitable, seeing him as a man who did his best in circumstances beyond his control, and who served a republic which he did not like to the best of his limited abilities. But here again the lightning conductor seems to be working as efficiently as it did in 1918. Hindenburg did nothing for the republic, and did much to weaken it. The bestiality that followed its demise was such that Ludendorff's bitter words were nearer the truth than the nobler expressions of understanding and even sorrow of his admirers and supporters.

What does Hindenburg's career tell us about soldiers and statesmen? His early career suggests that soldiers must always be under political control, and that they should not be allowed to make political decisions of enormous significance by pretending that they are making technical military judgements. At the same time the politicians must pursue rational and humane goals. His later career shows that the qualities needed of an army commander are not necessarily those of a successful political figure, and that the assumption that this is indeed so is based on faulty analogies between the roles of soldier and statesman. His career as President is proof of Brecht's remark that a nation is indeed to be pitied if it needs a great man. It is even more to be pitied when that great man turns out to be rather ordinary.

FURTHER READING

Gordon Craig, *The Politics of the Prussian Army: 1640-1945* (Oxford, 1955).

Andreas Dorpalen, *Hindenburg and the Weimar Republic* (Princeton, 1964).

Paul von Hindenburg, *Aus meinem Leben* (Leipzig, 1920).

Walther Hubatsch, *Hindenburg und der Staat* (Gottingen, 1966).

Martin Kitchen, *A Military History of Germany* (London, 1975).

Alfred Niemann, *Hindenburg: Ein Lebensbild* (Berlin, 1926).

Arthur Rosenberg, *Geschichte der deutschen Republik* (Karlsbad, 1935).

J.W. Wheeler Bennett, *Hindenburg the Wooden Titan* (London, 1936).

Franco

HUGH THOMAS

Of the generals in politics discussed in this book, Franco has surely had a more decisive effect on his own country than any other man. He led a successful revolt in his middle forties and remained the ruler of his country for almost the next forty years. That may be unusual in the twentieth century. It is a frequent story, though, in most recorded history, even if Franco, unlike most monarchs of his achievements in the past, has not sought to establish a dynasty: at the moment he is content with a family, though it is one which, shall we say, has not been wholly indifferent to the possibilities of profit under the crown.

Franco was in the Spanish Army for twenty-five years from 1911 to 1936. He had three years as generalissimo in the Civil War, 1936-39. Since 1939, he has had 36 years as Head of State, during most of which time he was head of government (until 1973).

Franco was in fact already a general when Byng left Canada and before Hindenburg was President. He was Head of State throughout the terms of office of Eisenhower and de Gaulle. No other Head of State now living and in power has been in authority longer than Franco has, by a long chalk. Indeed, I think his nearest rival must now be Tito, almost ten years his junior. He bridges more than two epochs and those who say his day is now done should remember that his father died at 87 and his grandfather at 92. He is, too, believed last year to have said to his elder brother Nicolas — now 85 — 'Remember, Nicolas, in the Franco family, we die in strict order of seniority of birth.'

Nor is Franco's rule in Spain simply a matter of longevity: during his time, Spain has undergone an industrial revolution and a major economic and social upheaval. This has been the most important event in Spain's history since the discovery of the Americas. Of course, it may be suggested that this achievement had nothing to do with Franco. Few would say that George III had much to do with the industrial revolution in England. Still, times have changed. The Head of State and government must have been a factor. I am of the view that Carlyle is nearer the mark than Marx in respect of the role of great men in the twentieth century — whatever the situation was in the past. Successive ministers or secretaries brought Franco plans for the creation of a new fishing fleet, the establishment of a chain of State hotels, a State holding company to stimulate investment, the framework of a modern road system, the continuation of large irrigation plans. Decisions were taken. A combination of factors was of course responsible for Spain's industrial transformation. These no doubt included the autarchy forced on Spain by the Second World War and the subsequent demand in northern Europe for Spanish labour, as well as tourism. This major change in Spanish life could certainly have occurred under other leaders, other régimes, at a different pace, and might have come in the 1960s, anyway, given Europe's revival and Spain's geographical position. Still, Franco was the chairman, let us say, of the country's advance. One can point to the relative lack of development in Portugal to be reminded that Spain might not have advanced.

Whatever happens to Spain after Franco disappears and whatever happens to Franco's reputation, this change will be impossible to controvert, though people will, of course, point out that some of the plans carried to fruition under Franco — for example, the Potemkin-like Badajoz plan for economic development — were begun before he was heard of. But the essential point is that Spain will have to be regarded as one of those countries which, like Japan, Germany, perhaps Brazil, have industrialised under a right-wing authoritarian structure, rather than under a democratic system (as other countries of northern Europe have, along with North America) or a socialist one (in the manner of Russia).

Two other preliminary points: we can argue here as to whether Franco is or is not responsible for these events, but we cannot make a decision because the evidence is not available. It is too near. The minutes of Franco's Cabinets presumably exist but no historian has seen them. Not a single Minister in any of Franco's governments since 1939 has written any account of how decisions have been taken. The absence of published memoris or diaries is remarkable. Perhaps political diarising and democracy go hand in hand. It may be hard to have to write notes about discussions as to whether or not a death sentence is approved even if one were to vote for a reprieve.

A second point is that, whether or not Franco's role has been itself decisive in that decisive change, he fits into a political structure which was not of his making. Looking back over the last sixty years since the First World War, one can see that Spain's entry into the modern world has been by and large authoritarian. The government which General Franco still heads was founded not in 1939, nor 1936, but in 1923, perhaps even in 1919. In that year, the country was on the edge of revolution, inspired by an incandescent anarchist working-class movement, a strong separatist movement in Catalonia, and unrest in the Army, partly caused by defeats in Morocco. The result was the nomination of a sanguinary general, Martínez Anido, as civil governor of Barcelona. He was determined to smash the revolutionary workers. Despite the outbreak of virtual civil war in Barcelona he was successful. Some months after he had given up his post, that same military experiment was tried, as a result of another Moroccan crisis, in the whole of Spain.

That was the seven-year dictatorship of General Primo de Rivera. Martínez Anido was Minister of the Interior. Primo de Rivera was followed by two less effective officers. These men worked under the king, and Spain was then a monarchy, but, even so, it was a military régime — if more tolerant, it must be said, than it ever was under Franco, even than it is in 1975. The Republic came in 1931, it is true, and, for two and a half years, there was, in the face of right-wing surprise and disorganisation, a left-of-centre government. But only for two and a half years. The succeeding right-wing governments of 1933-36 were constitutional but they enabled the clock to be turned back in a variety of ways, particularly on the land, where the government of the left had aroused expectations by radical legislation.

From February 1936 until the Civil War in July of that year, the country had a nominally centre government, but it was disobeyed by both right and left. One can even argue that, with armed gangs of young men of all political colours very active, the Civil War really began in the spring of 1936. After July, Spain collapsed into anarchy, to be revived as authoritarian with both camps tending to be totalitarian. This is the background against which Franco's régime must be judged. The men who started the rising in 1936 were carrying on from what Primo de Rivera had done in the 1920s but more brutally, for the lesson which they had learned from Primo de Rivera's fall was that, in the twentieth century, a despot has to be brutal, even if he might want to be enlightened.

To conclude this part of the argument: Spain has had an authoritarian government for over fifty years, even if for a short time it was constitutional. A real progressive government lasted two and a half years, if you exclude the revolutionary Republic in the Civil War which became steadily more totalitarian in character. Franco did not create the system. He inherited it. And it is no surprise that his first Minister of the Interior was Martínez Anido, the same ex-civil governor of Barcelona who was Primo de Rivera's.

Franco personally comes from a long line of naval administrators. Service to the State was in his blood on both sides of the family. Franco was intended for the Navy but, being born in 1892, he reached the moment to enter the naval cadet school at a bad time. There was no room for him and he had to break family tradition and enter the infantry academy. This was doubly important, both for its effect on Franco's attitude to that family tradition and for the fact that he found himself a would-be naval man in a military school.

Franco was brought up in an atmosphere of national humiliation after the Spanish-American war, particularly noticeably at El Ferrol, the late eighteenth-century naval base built by King Charles III, in which he lived as a child and which ran down fast after 1898. Franco's father was a drunken philanderer, while his mother was pious — appropriately she died in 1934, on the first lap of a pilgrimage to Rome. (The father left home and went to live in Madrid with a mistress about the time that Franco went to the Toledo infantry academy.) Perhaps this atmosphere helped to make Franco puritanical, reserved and intolerant.

Next, so far as influences on Franco are concerned, Franco is a

Gallego — a native, that is, of Galicia — a soft, green, poor
country on the north-west of Spain proverbially held by
Castillians to breed cautious, clever, patient, canny people —
Scotsmen on the make, as it might be said in England or
Canada. Galicia has contributed many outstanding politicians
in this country.

Finally, in respect of personal influences, Franco as a child
was slight as well as short, and must have wished to
compensate for innumerable jokes or bullying as a result by
seeking the 'bubble reputation' in the war in Morocco, where he
went very soon after taking his commission.

The Spanish Army was a political one. There was a tradition
of military intervention in Spanish politics in the nineteenth
century. Many officers at the turn of the century were known as
freemasons, liberals, republicans, Carlists and, later on, even
socialists. One or two officers were even friendly to anarchism.
There were also strong personal cliques so that many generals
would have a whole *camarilla* or team of followers whose
promotion prospects depended on them. The Spanish Army
was top-heavy: there were many, too many, officers per enlisted
man. Most of the time, it is true, in Franco's childhood and
youth, the Army kept out of overt political action. But the
threat of military intervention was always there. Would
General Weyler 'pronounce'? Was there a chance of General
Polavieja siding with the Carlists to overthrow the
constitutional monarchy?

The question of why so many soldiers have played such a
large part in politics in Spanish-speaking countries since 1800
is, I am glad to say, too large a one to deal with here in detail.
Glad, since it is a subject upon which none will agree. Is it to do
with the relation of men and women in Spain, the dominance of
the mother in the house, the freedom of the father outside, the
inevitable conversion of everyone to become or be made a
caudillo if they have achieved anything at all? (That excellent
Colombian novelist, Gabriel Garcia Marquez, told me last
winter that he had come to live in London not simply because
he liked the *degringolade* of our city in shambles and under the
fire of Irish bombs — but because where he lived in Mexico
people kept asking him to lead deputations.) Is it to do with the
Spanish empire or even with the Spanish language? At all
events, psychology and Inquisitors probably have a

contribution to make as historians must reluctantly recognise as they hear so often of wives of officers berating their husbands for inaction in some crisis or another — 'I do not understand, Miguelito, how you and the Army can stand aside and watch these gangsters, these outlaws, these wolves, these destroyers of the family. . .'.

Another important influence on Franco was the war in Morocco. As their share of the grab for Africa and as a means of keeping the French away from their southern coasts, and in order to profit from Moroccan mines, the Spaniards determined to conquer north Morocco as a protectorate. The will of Isabella the Catholic was remembered about 1900, just when the last memories of the American empire had passed away: and that will had said Spain's destiny lay in Africa. The war went on for eighteen years. Most of the time, Franco was there, at first fighting with the *regulares,* Moorish native troops — the Spaniards' sepoys — under Spanish officers: afterwards with the Foreign Legion, of which he became the third commander, a body of well-paid ruffians, mostly Spanish, modelled on the French Foreign Legion, and founded by Colonel Millan Astry, an officer of legendary courage and luck expressed by his one arm, black patch over the eye and few fingers on his only good hand. (The glorious mutilated one was incidentally the only possible surrogate father Franco might ever have had — the only Byng in his life, as Professor Graham would say.)

Franco's exploits in Morocco made him legendary for bravery, coolness in action and, oddly, when his subsequent record as a supreme commander is considered, for recklessness. I think he really did ride into action on a white horse. Franco became, of course, known as a member of that group of officers called the *africanistas*, who considered themselves new *conquistadors*, men who were writing 'a glorious page' in Spanish history by capturing 'sacred Xauen'. There was some basis for this fantasy, since they won the war, with the help of the French. That generation of officers, of whom Franco was one of the heroes, were nevertheless the first to bring back a Spanish victory from a colonial war for many generations. How obvious that, after a year or two of peace, they should begin to feel that they had a role to play in politics, particularly when the system seemed to be again collapsing!

Franco was known in Morocco in other ways: at that time the

protectorate seemed to some, such as Sergeant Barea, who well describes the atmosphere, as one huge brothel. Franco never joined the drinking, wenching officers of Tetuan or Ceuta. He sat alone in his tent reading, it is said, works of political theory, occupied at that time by neither *mujer no misa*, neither women nor mass, as his pious biographers hasten to add.

One further occurrence influencing Franco's political evolution was the Republic's Army reforms. The progressive Minister of War, Manuel Azaña, desired to improve the efficiency, as well as to cut the cost of the Army. He offended the officers in several ways: Franco's own new military academy at Saragossa was closed down, the national flag was changed — here compare Professor Kitchen on Hindenburg — the rank of captain general abolished, the initiation ceremony of kissing the flag also abolished, the corps of military chaplains wound up — rationalistic actions certain to offend a ritual-conscious traditional cadre of officers.

Given Franco's position as the youngest general, the social circumstances of his career, his favour with the ex-King Alfonso, it was natural that he should begin to be spoken of as a possible leader for a military intervention against a left-wing government. He acted as chief of staff to an expeditionary force which put down a left-wing revolution in Asturias in 1934. People said — Stay there. Franco's youth made him particularly attractive to younger officers and that also commended him to the young Fascists who were beginning to play a part in Spanish politics. But he nevertheless was not associated with the early monarchist plots active against the Republic. He did not take part in the Sanjurjo rising of 1932, a sort of Spanish Kapp *putsch*. Nor did he seem to have a following of his own.

1936 was the crucial year for Franco, as for others in the then deeply-divided Spanish Army. Franco toyed with the idea of a right-wing *coup* when the Popular Front won the elections in February, but he hesitated. When a military plot was finally mounted, Franco again hesitated to the end. 'With Franquito or without Franquito we're going to rise,' said one angry general. Once the die was cast, however, he acted swiftly, to take over control of the insurrectionary Foreign Legion and Moroccan troops, transport them as best he could to the peninsula, and even to approach the German Government for help. The

Germans were impressed enough with him — Admiral Canaris had apparently known him in Morocco — that they insisted that the weapons that they agreed to send should go to him, and to no other general. That was certainly one reason for the ease with which Franco established himself as the single supreme commander of the rebel forces only two months after the war had begun. By a sleight of hand, he and his friends succeeded in getting for him cilivian power as well as military. He was Head of State as well as generalissimo by October 1936.

How this was achieved is still a little- unclear. There was pressure, as might be imagined, to have a single commander. Franco was the obvious man for that. The titular leader of the rising was already dead in an air crash, probably because he had insisted on taking his full dress uniforms which weighed down his Puss Moth aircraft. (A cautionary tale for would-be rebel generals.) Franco's other possible rivals disqualified themselves in one way or another — General Mola, who had co-ordinated the plot against the Republic, was disliked by monarchists as being too radical, and hated by conventional officers as having once been a policeman. Then there was General Quiepo de Llano who with his gravelly, whisky voice was showing himself a brilliant war broadcaster. (The Spanish War pioneered several such technological innovations for military purposes.) But Quiepo de Llano was old, no field commander and something a joke. Franco, a favourite of King Alfonso, had served the Republic well till the last minute. He was, as I say, the obvious choice for military *caudillo*. The problem is how he gained civil as well as military power. A friend of his wrote out the decree deciding that. Some officers opposed it. They were talked out of it. One of them, Cabanellas, rightly predicted: 'I knew Franco in Morocco. Depend upon it, if you give him powers as head of government as well as supreme commander of the army, he will stay till he is dead.' An accurate prediction. Incidentally, Franco cleverly varied the wording of his office till the end of the war. Monarchists thought him a temporary head of government, who would restore the King after the victory. Fascists could see him as the *caudillo*, the *jefe*, the Spanish equivalent of Duce.

Franco's victory in the Civil War was partly made possible by the fact that, in what turned out to be a conventional war, the ex-veterans of the Moroccan war were better soldiers than their opponents. Partly, the material which the right got from Germany and Italy (though no more substantial than what the left got from Russia) was more imaginatively used than that which their enemies got. Franco also showed himself an intelligent diplomat — for example, with the Texas oil company whose chief, Captain Rieber, assured him all the oil which he needed on credit. In fact, the right in the Civil War got all their material on credit; their friends abroad therefore gave more and more in the hope that victory would pay their bills. The Republic settled their account in gold with the Russians in advance. Stalin therefore felt free to cut off help when convenient to him. A serious reflection, surely, on the inadequacy of traditional business morals.

Franco in the Civil War was also able to satisfy the increasingly vociferous demands of a frightened middle class for a heroic leadership, at a time when they needed little to push them over from defensive conservatism into Fascism. As a soldier Franco was criticised by those who felt that his response to any small attack of winning back what was lost, come what may, whether or not he had to abandon another campaign, showed excessive caution. Also, the Spanish monarchists think that he prolonged the war in order to consolidate his political position. For this, there is no evidence. At all events, Franco ended up as a victorious conqueror who had saved Spain from Communism in the 'last crusade'. From then on, he behaved more like a monarch to the East than any mere king of the West. The ceremony, the rigid insistence on etiquette, the Moroccan escort, the secrecy of the Government and the rareness of personal appearances, as well as the residence outside Madrid at the hunting lodge of El Pardo, made Sir Samuel Hoare's comparison of Franco with a Sultan apposite.

I've mentioned Fascism, and in the course of the war the alliance of right-wing Spaniards did put their case in terms close to those of Fascism or, as they might have put it, the 'language of empire'. A study of the Press in white Spain between 1936 and 1939 and even between 1939 and 1942 or 1943, shows that innumerable Nazi or Mussolinian symbols, catchwords and even institutions were introduced into Spain. Heroic leadership I mentioned, but there were also the promises of regeneration, the appeals to a remote past (the spirit of a new *Reconquista)*, the denunciations of democratic decadence, the ludicrous renaming of streets and oratorios that characterised the cultural renaissance or counter-renaissance, of Fascism. France, in particular, was the scapegoat, the enemy, perhaps even more than Russia and 'the Reds', since France could be represented as playing a malign note of seducing Spanish virtue not just for ten but for two hundred years, since the French Revolution. The hostility to France was such that all French words had to disappear from menus. Even 'ragoût' became 'Madrid stew'.

Even so, Franco's Fascism was opportunist. He was too clever to believe that Mussolini's strutting was any substitute for organised military government and in practice Franco never hoped to revive any more of the Spanish empire than to smash Catalonia.

Franco also was very clever in disposing of those committed, sincere Spanish Fascists who might have been a threat to his pragmatism. Manuel Hedilla, for instance, the leader of the Falange after the death of that small group's founder, José Antonio Primo de Rivera (son of the old dictator): Hedilla was framed, gaoled, condemned to death and, after that punishment was commuted, spent several years in prison for no reason save that he was a threat. (One can contrast the much greater difficulty the Republicans had with their dissidents in the Civil War.)

Despite many broken promises, and the holding of a referendum in 1947 on the question of whether Spain should formally become a monarchy — the answer was yes — Franco has held on to power ever since the war, occasionally seeming to yield to one pressure group or another (Opus Dei, Catholic Action, the Falange, the USA), but only agreeing, in the late 1960s, to adopt a grandson of the late King Alfonso as his heir, and even appointing his first Prime Minister only in 1973.

One other eastern element in Franco's methods of using power must be mentioned. His is a cold temperament. As Isaiah Berlin said of Sir Oliver Franks, he is like the ocean: the deeper you go, the colder it gets. Franco is utterly humourless. He came to believe that his mission was to 'clean up' Spain from the heresies of socialism, freemasonry and liberalism — all the products of the accursed nineteenth century, and northern European democracy. The murders on the revolutionary side in the Civil War steeled his heart further. The consequence was a

systematic repression affecting thousands, probably hundreds
of thousands. The executions only abated when it became clear
about 1942 that the Allies would win the war. By then, too, the
tempers of the Spanish middle class, which had fully supported
this repression, had cooled somewhat, and the follies of the
Spanish version of Fascism, so far as propaganda was
concerned, vanished. Franco was responsible for signing more
death sentences than any other ruler in Spanish history, or
probably, indeed, than any other ruler in European history
other than Hitler and Stalin.

This will clearly mark his reputation indefinitely if and when
his system is overthrown. As it is, the years of repression after
the war form an unforgettable period of despair cutting off the
present from the happier past and even the excitements of the
war — a time whose mood is well captured by a beautiful film
made in Spain — *The Spirit of the Beehive*.

Franco is not a man of ideas. He despises them and hates
intellectuals. The endless talk of café politicians appals him just
as it did, say, Lenin. One must admit that, embarrassing
though it may seem, a lack of principle is a good preparation for
diplomacy. Franco was clever to be able to keep out of the
Second World War, clever to let down his old Axis friend, clever
to be able to give help to the Allies from the moment that they
seemed likely to win, clever to mobilise Spanish nationalism in
1945 to resist any attempt by those same Allies, as they
proposed, to impose a settlement from outside, with the help of
the Bourbon family. Franco ensured his régime's survival after
the war, during the must successful use of UN sanctions ever
practised, by an arrangement with Perón. Then came friendship
with the US and the virtual entry of Spain into the Western
alliance. In 1962, an American general said that he thought
Spain the best ally the US had. I suspect that that was true, if
it meant the least trouble with local public opinion, the speed
with which decisions were taken, and the dedication which the
Spaniards of the régime still had to the anti-Communist
crusade. I can't see that Franco could have done much better
for Spain internationally than he has done. He has not actually
secured Spain's entry into the European Economic Community
but perhaps that is as much because he doesn't really want to
as because we don't want him. In other elements of foreign
policy the Spaniards since the war have been quite clever in

avoiding commitments and making an advantage of necessity. Spain for example is a friend of the Arabs — no Israeli Embassy in Madrid — but US transport planes refuelled at Torrejon in the war of 1973.

Franco has also been always clever with the pressure groups that have existed under the surface in his authoritarian structure. Of course, I repeat, he had that great prestige as the victorious commander who saved the middle class from destruction and he could also play on that 'anxiety to survive', as the Spaniards put it, which characterises people after they have only just stopped fighting. Even so there were always Falangists who wanted to make Spain more Fascist, Christian Democrats who wanted to open out towards post-war Europe, monarchists who wanted a restoration, even old churchmen, such as Cardinal Segura of Seville, who disliked the materialism which he believed the US alliance might bring. Franco threaded his way here most skilfully just as if he was negotiating with the fifty-six tribes in Morocco in his youth. In doing this, he created a new class of public servants who have become known as *franquistas* — people who owe everything to the regime, have no loyalties outside it, neither Fascist nor monarchist, nor particularly Catholic, by whom Spain is still governed. Possibly, though Franco has been quite a good selector of men, these *franquistas* may be the worst of the general's legacies. All dominant men create a habit of mind. Franco has endowed procrastination, opportunism and caution with a kind of halo which may seem to fit very badly on Spain when he, the grand designer, the very Dior of procrastination, has gone.

Only recently, admittedly, have things seemed to be escaping Franco's control. The first occasion was when, in the late 1960s, the lay order, Opus Dei, acquired a stranglehold on the State, as a result of Franco's reliance on Admiral Carrero Blanco, a submarine commander, who was his secretary, general factotum and then Prime Minister. The second occasion was when, after the blowing up of Carrero and the consequent swift eclipse of the Opus, the new Prime Minister, Arias Navarro, promised a liberalisation of political life which he has not been able to carry through but which certainly aroused intellectual expectations.

Another element in Franco's technique of government is that dismissed Ministers almost never come back. There have been many changes of Cabinet since 1939. Some people have remained Ministers a long time. Some have moved from one Ministry to another. One in one instance — that of José Solis — has anyone returned to power as Minister having ceased to be one.

But, you are still asking, despite my statements about Franco's hatred of ideas, what does Franco believe in? What is his view of politics? I need to repeat myself. Brought up to despise politicians, Franco was given some reason to support that view in his early manhood. The recent candid remarks by the Portuguese Minister of Information as to how tired he and his brother officers were of political parties, after less than a year of them, might have been drafted by Franco. The political crisis of the Republic in the 1930s was manifested by many political changes which discredited democracy. Franco has sought to abolish politics. He is certainly a monarchist partly because Alfonso XIII was kind to him, partly because he thinks a monarchy will keep the country together, partly because he likes being king himself. He has never been any good at speaking in public — his high-pitched voice is bad for oratory and he could never have come to the top in a system in which the spoken word was important. (Perhaps he is an apt visitation on Spain which in the past had a surfeit of orators.) That negativism of his seemed to work for a long time: about 1953, he told a foreign journalist that he could never understand why people in the past had made such a fuss about the difficulty of running Spain. He personally found it very easy. I fear he is a little complacent.

For now the plaster cast of dictatorship has lifted a little, all the old wounds still seem to be there: Catalonia, the Basque country, the working class's desire for a millenarian solution, even the problem of the Army in politics. The new constitution can hardly survive after Franco's death. His own use of that constitution has made the task of his adopted successor, Prince Juan Carlos, immeasurably more difficult. By procrastinating, he has ruined the best chances of countless well-intentioned, democratic, forward-looking people who reject authoritarian solutions but who may be swept aside. The most obvious successor State to Franco may be either a new even more authoritarian structure of the right, headed by those who resisted successfully the present Prime Minister's efforts at liberalisation; or an equally intransigent illiberal authoritarianism of the Communist left, whose anti-Francoism would no doubt be vociferous, even if it actually derived some of its strength from the Francoist structure. The path to an open society is thus still overgrown, tortuous and, in some places, barely recognisable even as a path. And, despite radical changes in the social structure (for example in the role of women, in the Church, in morals), Spain is still recognisably an authoritarian society.

By and large, I am inclined to give Franco ('the least straightforward man I ever met' — John Whitaker), much of the credit for the economic transformation of Spain. But I blame him not only for his cruelty, but for his neglect to create a political system which would give security against the abuse of power in the future — security even to those who supported him in the past. Had he supported the attempts of, say, Manuel Fraga and José Solis in the 1960s, as well as Arias Navarro's, Spain could have looked forward much more self-confidently. Now there is doubt, as there is throughout the Mediterranean. The difficulties are exacerbated by the energy crisis, the return of Spanish workers from abroad, increasing inflation and unemployment. The days of the miracle seem over. The best definition of a tyrant is one who neglects to make proper provision for the future. The cap fits Franco well.

FURTHER READING

Gerald Brenan, *The Spanish Labyrinth* (Cambridge, 1943).
Raymond Carr, *Spain, 1808-1939* (London, 1966).
Brian Crozier, *Franco* (London, 1967).
George Hills, *Franco* (London, 1967).
Stanley Payne, *The Politics of the Military in Modern Spain* (Stanford, 1967).

Lord Byng in Canada

ROGER GRAHAM

Soldiers as statesmen: Paul von Hindenburg, Francisco Franco, Dwight Eisenhower, Charles de Gaulle and Julian Byng. Julian *who?* I think it is certain that Viscount Byng, a modest man, would be astonished and somewhat embarrassed to find himself being considered under such a heading and included among such company. For Byng, after all, was only a Governor General; even before the Imperial Conference of 1926 which, following hard on the famous constitutional crisis in Canada, undertook to define the nature and reduce the responsibilities of that office, a Governor General enjoyed comparatively little scope for statesmanship of an active and public kind. As Lord Byng expressed it to his old friend John Buchan shortly after he and Lady Byng ensconced themselves in Rideau Hall, the Vice-regal residence, 'We have settled down — myself as Govr Genl i.e. a Governor who doesn't govern and a General who cannot generalize, and my 'better ½' as Governess General — but we are both happy. . . .'[1]

Byng's stay in Canada is chiefly remembered for the fact that he had the misfortune, shortly before his retirement, to confront the most difficult situation faced by a Governor General since Confederation. His response to that situation is, I suppose, his chief claim to statesmanship. But so much ink has been spilled over the constitutional crisis, the story has been told so often, the questions it raised have been so thoroughly analysed and so much debated, that there is no need or excuse for me to offer here yet another treatment of the subject.[2] Instead I shall concentrate on the years before 1926, and especially on the relationship that grew between Byng and Mackenzie King. If much of what follows seems trivial, with little relevance to the subject of soldiers as statesmen, it is not only because it is largely based on King's extraordinary diary. The circumscriptions which had grown up around the office Byng held doomed him, at least until the royal prerogative came dramatically into play in 1926, to perform a role about as far removed as it could be from, let us say, the starring part in *la politique de la grandeur*. He could do little more in Canada than prompt the stage actors from the wings, hoping they would take the cue, while confining himself in public to what Buchan, one of his successors, was later to call 'governor generalities'.

There is, however, no doubt about the credentials as a soldier of Lieutenant-General the Honourable Sir Julian H.G. Byng, KCB, KCMG, MVO, later Baron and still later Viscount Byng of Vimy. He began his military service as a young cavalry officer in India in the early 1880s and later fought in the South African War. In 1912 he was made commander of the army of occupation in Egypt, whence he returned to England shortly after the outbreak of war in 1914 to lead a cavalry division to the western front, subsequently being put in command of the Cavalry Corps.

Shortly after that promotion he was despatched to the Dardanelles as a corps commander and returned to France early in 1916 in the same capacity. At the end of May in that year he was transferred to take charge of the Canadian Corps and just over twelve months later was advanced to command of the Third Army. In 1919 he was given a barony in recognition of his wartime service, which one gathers was genuinely distinguished, and at the age of 57, retired from the Army, he was ready for suitable peacetime employment.

In those days a Governor General was customarily nominated by the Colonial Office, with the Government of the Dominion concerned having the right to veto a proposed appointment. In the spring of 1920 it was suggested to the King by certain 'responsible Canadians' of identity now unknown that Lord Byng, presumably because of his association with the Canadian Corps, would be an appropriate successor to the Duke of Devonshire, whose term would expire a year later. Byng was sounded out and he indicated his willingness.[3] If those 'responsible Canadians' had spoken the mind of their Government, its mind had changed by early 1921 when it came time to make a decision. It had other preferences and only when those proved to be unrealisable did Byng, the first choice of the

Colonial Office all along, get the job by default.[4] Since Canada had never before had to make do with a lowly baron but recently raised to the peerage, it may be that some more exalted personage was desired, though as a son of the 2nd Earl of Strafford and, on his mother's side, grandson of a Duke of Devonshire, Byng was not exactly a stranger to the aristocracy. A more probable explanation is the Meighen Government's belief that someone with a civilian background would be preferable to a military man, no matter how esteemed. The war to end war was over, and passions aroused in Canada during and because of it were dying down. The appointment of a British general might freshen memories of conflicts that were best forgotten.

As it turned out, Byng did not at all match the popular stereotype of the general as a spit-and-polish authoritarian. During the War, it is said, he was notorious for presiding over the worst officers' mess in Europe, a judgement confirmed and stated to his face by King George V during a tour of inspection.[5] Upon the arrival of Their Excellencies in Ottawa, Mackenzie King remarked approvingly on the noticeable absence of 'side' in Lord Byng[6] and found him to be 'very retiring, a little standoffish and shy, a feeling I can well appreciate as I feel it myself.'[7] Given his abhorrence of the military, King must have been pleased to hear Byng speak 'of desiring to get away from the War in all public talk, to cease referring to ourselves as "heroes" ';[8] and doubtless he was happy to be assured by the Governor that 'no one had been less military than himself', that on occasion at Government House 'he only wore the uniform because it was the best clothes he had.'[9] This last was entirely believable; he bought his 'civvies' at Moss Brothers. Attired in a Moss Brothers ensemble, with a badly frayed felt hat on his head, his feet encased in a pair of disgusting old white rubber boots presented to him by a Yukon miner, he would set off on his frequent walks around Parliament Hill accompanied by a mortified aide-de-camp. One of his ADCs, Colonel H. Willis-O'Connor, upon being told with some glee by His Excellency that he had found 'a short cut into town through a succession of backyards', warned him that 'he might be arrested at the instance of some indignant housewife who, seeing his shabby clothing, would mistake him for a common trespasser.'[10]

Byng's first words upon arriving in Canada were to confess his inexperience in the kind of work he was now taking up and to predict that he would make mistakes.[11] No doubt he did make mistakes, though not necessarily all the ones Mackenzie King accused him of, and these sprang from his not very surprising unfamiliarity with the niceties of constitutional practice and the strangeness, for a man accustomed to decide, to lead and to command, of the position in which he found himself. Byng desired to exert some influence, to do some good for Canada, to which he felt a genuine attachment, and he sometimes chafed under the restrictions inherent in his position.

The office had two aspects at that time and they were not always easy to separate from each other. As an agent of the British Government and a channel of communication between it and the Government of Canada, Byng experienced little difficulty, at least as his Prime Minister saw it. On such issues as the Chanak crisis of 1922 and the signing of the Halibut Treaty of 1923 he strongly supported the stands taken by Mackenzie King, though he was baffled (as were many others) by the tortuous arguments King employed in opting out of the Treaty of Lausanne and not altogether pleased by his ingrained suspicion of anything smacking of Empire solidarity. However, Byng readily agreed that these were matters for the Canadian Government to decide upon.

In any event, he thought of himself not as an agent of the British Government, but simply as the representative of His Majesty.[12] It was in discharging this side of his responsibilities that he found himself in some hot water, not all of it of his own boiling, it must be added, and, if King's diary can be believed, his chief mistake was in allowing too close and personal a connection to develop between himself and his First Minister. That is said without precise knowledge of what ordinarily passes between sovereigns or governors general and their advisers, though one is inclined to dismiss as an exaggeration the dictum in a student examination paper some years ago that 'It is the duty of the British Prime Minister to have daily intercourse with the Queen.' But if the diary is reliable evidence, Byng was very ill-advised, it seems to me, in seeing so much of and talking so much of Mackenzie King, in not keeping their relationship somewhat more distant and formal.

The qualification about the diary as evidence is, of course, important because one must rely so heavily on it in examining the association of the two men and because its credibility as a record of what was actually said and done, as distinct from how King rendered or what he read into what was said and done, is the most puzzling evidential problem facing students of twentieth-century Canadian politics, especially if they lack a solid grounding in psychology or psychiatry. In an interesting recent exercise in Eriksonian psycho-history it has been argued that King found in Lord Byng the surrogate father for whom he had a deep need, his own father, even his grandfather Mackenzie and such politician heroes and patrons as Sir William Mulock and Sir Wilfrid Laurier having failed to satisfy all the demanding requirements of the association he craved. He needed someone of standing and prestige between whom and himself there could be a strong bond of trust and affection, someone he could truly admire, in whom he could confide and who would support him through thick and thin, and yet against whose parental authority he must eventually assert himself in order to resolve his identity crisis and establish his dominance.[13] King himself, as one would expect, did not see Lord Byng as a surrogate father. In one of the numerous lessons in constitutional government he gave His Excellency, he offered his own ultimate definition of their relationship: 'I told him our relations as P.M. & G.G. were much like a couple about to be married either "love me all in all or not at all"....'[14] Upon hearing which Byng must surely have thought to himself, 'Dear me, how very odd!'

The psychological approach, to which, needless to say, there is much more than my highly condensed paraphrase would indicate, is suggestive and in some ways persuasive, although at the end where King turns into the father and Byng into the son one becomes a bit confused. However, one who is too ignorant of psychology to essay psycho-history can only remark that Mackenzie King was uncommonly inclined to 'egocentrise' his associations with other people, to interpret their words and actions from the standpoint of what they revealed about attitudes to him personally or to his opponents. Following the public greeting to the Byngs on Parliament Hill he wrote a revealing comment in his diary: 'What was noticeable to me today was the great deference of many of the ministers towards myself and the notice taken of men by the crowds as I went by.'[15]

King conceived an instant liking for Baron Byng which, judging by what he told both the diary and the House of Commons, grew into genuine admiration and affection that survived, but by no means wholly unimpaired, their strenuous passage-at-arms in 1926. It was, though, admiration and affection strongly dependent on Byng's favourable attitude to him, on his likemindedness, his agreeableness, his desire to be 'helpful' and his preference for King as an adviser. The diary is liberally sprinkled with such statements as the following:

> . . .I received a very cordial letter from His Excellency. . . . It begins 'My dear Prime Minister.' I believe our relations are going to be very pleasant, happy and mutually beneficial.
> His Ex. could not have been friendlier or more of a like mind to myself.
> The Governor General (is) a true friend and noble companion.
> Lord Byng is truly anxious to be of real help and is most kindly and generously disposed towards myself.
> . . .I do not think he likes Meighen. . . .
> He is very friendly, wants to help. . . .
> He is a true friend, a man of great spiritual strength and power.[16]

Another feature of King's egocentricity, as the observation after the Parliament Hill reception suggests, was his tendency to magnify both the reality and the significance of other people's language and behaviour as they concerned him. He was apt to be excessively grateful or incensed, like the character in Dryden's *Absalom and Achitophel,* 'So over-violent or over-civil,/That every man, with him, was God or Devil.' This was most clearly demonstrated, although Byng himself never became a devil in King's eyes, in the difficult political situation resulting from the 1925 election and the constitutional crisis that ensued.

But to return to the point of this lengthy digression about the credibility of the diary: one is bound to suspect that it is a distorting mirror reflecting an overdrawn image of King's many meetings with His Lordship, of what they said to one another, a depiction of the nearly ideal relationship — until their first serious falling out in 1925 — as it existed in the mind of Mackenzie King. Did His Excellency, for example, actually say to King in their first interview in September 1921, 'Mr King, I want to put myself in your hands. . . . I shall be glad to have you speak very freely'?[17] Certainly that was a rather strange thing for a Governor General to say to the leader of the Opposition; had King heard that Byng had said it to Arthur Meighen after the positions of the two party leaders were reversed, he would have been furious. Or was Lord Byng, in what turns out to have been but one in a series of chats with members of Parliament and other Ottawa personages, simply trying to get acquainted and to lessen the snobbish exclusiveness which had surrounded his office in the past? Again, consider this excerpt from King's account of the interview in June 1926 at which his resignation as Prime Minister was received and accepted. 'He took my hands in his and said: "Mr. King, you know that I would much rather have you as Prime Minister than Mr. Meighen; you know that, do you not?" '[18] Would a Governor General, however innocent about constitutional practice and propriety, say such a thing, especially to a man who, as Lady Byng accurately described it to John Buchan, for three days in a row had 'insulted, bullied, threatened him, with everything he could think of' in an effort to have Parliament dissolved?[19] Perhaps so, or it may be that King had to believe that Byng preferred him to his hated rival. One cannot be sure, but there is reason to be sceptical.

Still, whatever reservations one may have about the diary as a record of events, there it is, the nearest Canadian equivalent of the White House tapes, and obviously it is not just a collection of imaginings. Keeping in mind the need to regard its contents sceptically, what does it tell us about Lord Byng in his capacity as representative of the King? Three things chiefly, I think: first, as already suggested, that he became too 'chummy' with his Prime Minister; secondly, that like most of his predecessors he attempted to influence policy in certain respects; and thirdly, that he was something of a babe in the woods where constitutional practice as well as Canadian politics and the party system were concerned. This latter deficiency has been emphasised and documented by Mackenzie King's official biographers but Byng himself does not seem to have been aware of it. In his opening interview with King before the 1921 election, he said:

> As to being a constitutional gov'r, I understand that, there will be little difficulty to keep on right lines. As to party politics, they are easily understood. I suppose the old parties here are much as they are in Eng. The one wants a little more 'Liberty', the other a little more law. There are Libs who are conservative and conservatives who are Liberal. With the Farmers one can understand it is the tariff.[20]

This unsophisticated view of the competing political forces King attempted to displace by his own equally simplistic and highly moralistic, not to say theological, conception of what the parties stood for. One doubts that Byng was overly impressed by that; he had a certain scorn for partisan politics and rivalries, believing that they stood in the way of getting important things done for Canada. In her autobiography Lady Byng stated this scorn more strongly, as she did most things, explaining that she and her husband had 'always shunned and detested politics', which one of King's biographers calls 'an extraordinary frame of mind for one who had chosen to live in that *milieu* for four or five years'.[21] However, Lord Byng's error lay, not in shunning politics — his ignorance of it diminished as time went by — but rather, judging by his conversations with King as recorded in the diary, in not retaining that degree of aloofness from the political *milieu* which a Governor General needs to have. That is, before the 1925 election upset the applecart, he gave King the impression, unintended though it may have been, of being disposed in his favour, of wanting him rather than his rival to succeed, in short, of being the partisan that King desired him to be. When that favourable disposition became, as King saw it, qualified and less certain following the election, as Byng repeatedly urged him to resign in deference to Meighen's stronger position in the new House of Commons, King reacted like a suddenly jilted suitor, with a mixture of sorrow and anger and very much afraid, though not wanting to admit it, that the cause of it all was 'another man'.

The anger, though, was directed less at Byng personally than at those surrounding him in Rideau Hall. '. . . There is no doubt,' wrote King, 'Tory influences are at his elbow day and night. . . . I am beginning to see clearly that Government House is a Tory preserve — it stands for privilege — The more I reflect the more I see the wisdom if it can be attained of having as Govr. Gen. some one of Liberal traditions and of prltry experience — not military or court circles.' But Byng himself, King still believed, was 'really anxious to do the right'.[22] The trouble was, apparently, that His Lordship did not always understand 'the right'; certainly he was mistaken in the stands he adopted on some constitutional points, and in some of the actions he took or failed to take. Perhaps, to be fair to him, almost any imaginable Governor General, civilian or soldier, liberal or conservative, with or without parliamentary experience, would not have been free from confusion in the situation that arose after the 1925 election and in dealing with that particular Prime Minister. Anyway, when the acid test came in late June 1926, Lord Byng made the right decision on the most important issue and, it may be, not altogether for the wrong reasons.

Let us look a little more closely at the rapport that developed between the two men as it is depicted in the diary, and also, for a moment, at the lack of rapport between King and Lady Byng. This was not without some significance because in the course of time King became convinced that Her Excellency was one of those who exemplified the Tory bias of Government House, that she had, in fact, lent herself and her influence with her husband to a Tory plot to oust him from power. His initial impressions of her were favourable, however. At the welcome on Parliament Hill he observed her 'naturalness and pleasantness' and thought she had 'an intellectual face, not a beauty at all, but a sensible woman.'[23] Shortly after moving into Laurier House he invited the Byngs over for tea by themselves, and it went well. Both of them graciously made the right noises as King proudly took them on a tour of the house. In his cherished top floor library they 'were both much taken with mother's picture by the fireside, and my bible,' they 'seemed genuinely interested' in the bed linens which he took care to show them and, while agreeing that 'the drawing-room was cold', they 'liked the morning-room and dear mother's bust.'[24] But King could never feel quite at ease with Lady Byng, a woman of

literary bent and volatile temperament. 'Find it a little difficult
to talk with her,' he noted, 'mostly because of a lack of subjects
and interests in common. She has not had the training or
background of the wives of previous G.G's but is most pleasant
and unconventional.'[25] Before very long, King discovered that
she was not so pleasant after all as he sensed, correctly, that she
actively disliked him. That realisation and his distaste for the
brittle, trivial table-talk at Rideau Hall, carried on in a style so
alien to his own, may account, along with his expressed desire
for a day in the week to himself, for his request to be excused
from what had become his customary regular attendance at
Sunday night supper with the Byngs and their staff. Of course
he was frequently invited after that and there were other
opportunities, such as their walks together around Rockcliffe,
for conversing with His Excellency.

King obviously attached real value and importance to these
numerous discussions with Lord Byng. After supper the two
would retire to the library and talk at length about a variety of
things: religion, international affairs, imperial relations,
Canadian politics and domestic policy and, of course,
constitutional monarchy and the office of Governor General.
Once they had an intense, tongue-clucking consultation about
the behaviour of the Prince of Wales during his recent visit to
Ottawa, behaviour so reprehensible that it provoked Byng into
forbidding His Royal Highness to visit Canada again while he
was Governor General.[26] It was usually in the course of writing
his account of these conversations that King would include one
of the admiring comments about Lord Byng quoted earlier.

What His Excellency reportedly had to say on one of these
general subjects, policy and politics in Canada, is apposite to
my point about his over-exposure to Mackenzie King, especially
when the talk got on to party tactics and electoral prospects as
it frequently did in 1924 and 1925. One could not seriously
object to his expressing opinions in private to the Prime
Minister about what government policy should be, even though
some of the issues touched upon were in dispute between the
opposing parties, provided that he did not try to impose them
on the unwilling adviser. King himself did not object to this as
long as Byng's views were in accord with his own general
desire, as they usually were. Subject to that condition, he found
the suggestions stimulating and helpful. For example, Byng

clearly had no use for the protective tariff and King, who was anxious to thwart Meighen's effort to make survival of the National Policy the overriding question of the hour, was doubtless pleased to hear His Excellency speak of 'no one caring about the tariff as an issue. . . .'[27] Byng, in fact, agreed 'that Reciprocity had been the right policy for Canada.'[28] Nor would King be averse, since it was consistent with his self-image as defender of the people against the 'interests', to being urged by Byng 'not to be afraid to fight the mffrs. ass'n and to do so in the open. He was quite outspoken on that,' wrote King, 'I am surprised he went so far.'[29] The tariff was objectionable because it raised the cost of living. Byng kept repeating that this was the theme the Government should emphasise. 'He counsels strongly doing something to reduce the cost of living, as something that will be understood by everyone, even if it involves a fight with the Mffrs. Associat'n. He would go so far as to say in speech from throne even if budget is not balanced for a year or two, we must keep down the cost of living because of lower costs in U.S. and danger of migration thitherward (*sic*).'[30] To sound that note about the budget must have caused Lord Byng a little anguish because he was as firm a believer in balanced budgets as Mackenzie King — and, for that matter, Arthur Meighen.

But His Lordship had a far grander programme to suggest than mere humdrum anti-protectionism and that sort of thing. It reflected his desire to be statesmanlike but at the same time his innocence of many of the complex constitutional and political realities in Canada. One infers from the sentiments attributed to him in King's diary that it arose in large part from his enthusiasm for western Canada, the young, dynamic part of the country that represented the bright future and also offered the best duck shooting he had every enjoyed. Byng laid out his plan in a general way before King early in 1924, 'His Excellency saying I had been so nice and helpful to him he wished he could help me if he were not doing what was wrong in making suggestions.' The diary continues its paraphrase of Byng's discourse:

He then spoke of a big policy 'Economic constructive development of natural resources and agric. — 2.Economy. 3. Immigration — if developed in a large way.' . . . would

win the young men from one end of Canada to another.
The young men were wanting leadership and eager for the
big thing. He did not believe in the 'Rideau Club' politics,
always of Sir John MacDonald (*sic*) & Sir Wilfried Laurier
they were both great men — great Empire Builders but
they were dead. We needed to develop our country & our
trade, get markets everywhere for what we can produce.
Get a large policy, not be afraid of having it too large. He
said being detached & looking on, he could see what the
young men were thinking, feeling & saying. He is right
about the need for a large constructive policy. I must get
down to this side of my work & that soon.[31]

Byng returned to this theme after another Sunday supper a
week later. 'Spoke of my taking a real lead in a bold policy of
development of resources & expansion of trade & of economy,
thought I was over modest, that the people wanted a leader &
would follow. He keeps emphasizing this note.'[32]

Whether or not Lord Byng was accurate in his reading of the
public mind, it was not very realistic to expect Mackenzie King
to take up the mantle of Macdonald and Laurier. Nor did
Byng's 'let's put our shoulders to the wheel and get on with it
for Canada' attitude, sincere though it unquestionably was,
reflect a very hard-headed appreciation of the actualities of the
situation. It was, perhaps, an attitude more typical of the
soldier than of a man accustomed to the subtleties and
complexities of political life. But he was trying to be helpful in
spurring the Prime Minister on, and in making the effort he did
no harm.

However, if the diary can be trusted, he did more than that:
he became almost an ally before the 1925 election, counselling
King on how to conduct his campaign, encouraging him and
commiserating with him when the election ended badly for the
Liberal Party. That apparent bias, indeed, showed through long
before Parliament was dissolved in September. During one of
their after-dinner chats in January, King recorded, His
Excellency 'spoke of my present position, as being on the crest
of a wave, with no real opposition. One party trying to get rid of
their leader and the other trying to find one. He thought I
would carry the country easily were an appeal to be made at
present.'[33] A month later this entry appeared: 'His Ex. thinks

there is no doubt the Govt. wd. carry the country if I appealed this summer & is inclined to think an early appeal — or rather appeal this year preferable to next.'³⁴ And at the end of March, this: 'He thinks we wd. lose in Maritimes, — also 3 or 4 seats in Quebec. Wd. gain from progressives in rural Ont. — lose in cities of Ont. including Ottawa, wd. gain in West — cannot say of B.C. thinks we will be sure to come back & shld. go this year.'³⁵ Baron Byng was not only becoming educated about party politics, he was beginning to sound like a political organiser.

Early in September, Byng reported to King on a visit to the West just concluded. 'His Ex. . . was very strong on my going West soon and spending much time there, not to bother with Maratimes *(sic)*. . . . He thought I wd. be returned. . . . He sd. the West was for me he thought. . . .'³⁶ Byng brought up the same idea a little later. Shortly after the election was announced he

> stressed again my going to the West, to the smaller places — said he thought I had made a mistake in giving the Maritime provinces any time. Was anxious I should come to him after elections with a following from the West that would make Canada a united country. . . From diff't remarks I gathered he thought it wd. be better for me not to go after Meighen so hard, not to attack him, but to keep to issue. Let Meighen do the 'dirty work.' I think he is right — but I hate a liar and a perverter of the truth.³⁷

So far so good, from the standpoint of King's satisfaction with Lord Byng's conduct as Governor General; so good, in fact, that Byng could tell Buchan in the spring of 1925: 'The Government's view out here is that my relations with them have been very happy and they hate the idea of change.' They 'have offered me an extension to practically any term I like. . .'.³⁸

The election in the fall and what it led to, however, seriously disturbed the harmonious association of His Excellency and Mackenzie King. Both of them had foreseen setbacks for the Liberals and the possibility that the Conservatives would win at least a plurality of seats, as in fact happened. Byng predicted to Buchan a few days before the polling that 'Meighen will probably have the largest party which would be larger if he were more popular but I am

doubtful if he will beat King if the latter unites the Liberals and
Progressives under one banner.'[39] This last remark seems to
bear out King's belief that the Governor agreed that he would
be entitled to meet the new Parliament as Prime Minister if the
Conservatives were short of a majority. King had raised the
point early in September. 'His Ex. . . . said I was the P.M. he
was there to accept my advice. I sd. I must be given my chance
to show what I can do in prlt. . . . His Ex. agreed.'[40] King was
therefore understandably taken aback when, at their first
interview following the election, Byng urged him to resign.

The interview started off well enough with Byng saying,
'Well, I can't tell you, my dear friend, how sorry I am for you'
and that 'he had hoped for better results for us in Manitoba. . .'.
However, when King recalled their earlier conversation about
his right to meet the new Parliament, Byng interrupted to press
the view that it would be more dignified and in King's larger
political interest for him to resign. This would prevent his being
accused of clinging to power and his having to bargain for the
support of the Progressives and Labourites. It 'would put me
on the crest of a wave in a very short time, . . . the West would
see its mistake & back me solidly, we would be rid of the third
parties. He returned to the "dignified" course. I agreed as to
this and . . . said I was sure His Ex. was right.' His colleagues,
said King, 'would probably oppose the idea, but I would be
firm. His Ex. sd. he hoped that (?) if the Cabinet opposed me I
wd. stand out. I said I would. . . . I felt a great mental relief as
His Ex. talked. . . .'[41]

The relief did not last long. Having talked to the Cabinet,
King changed his mind, informing Byng that he must advise
that Parliament be summoned at the earliest possible date and
asserting, correctly, that this would accord with British
precedent, since what counted was the confidence of the House
of Commons and not which party leader had the largest
following. Byng responded that he would 'be obliged to say that
while I accept your advice, I differ from you in opinion'. King
then had to explain that it would be quite out of order for a
Governor General to disagree publicly with his Prime Minister,
that 'qua Govr. Genl. he had no opinions. He could reject my
advice in which event I would resign.' Lord Byng was now
discovering that there were difficulties in being a constitutional
governor that had not occurred to him when he first arrived in

Ottawa. Finally he gave in and a statement was issued saying, with less than scrupulous accuracy, that he had been 'graciously pleased to accept' the advice given. To King this incident showed, as he told His Excellency (one imagines to the latter's surprise), 'that Governors coming out from Britain seemed almost invariably to side with the Tory party in Canada. I did not thing he intended to, but that wd. be the impression created, it wd. be bad for Imperial connection.' Still, King conceded, 'Lord Byng has certainly tried to be fair & just & has been fair & just. The natural Tory could not helping *(sic)* asserting itself in the feeling that the Govt. shld. resign and let the Tories come in, but this, I truly believe, was meant as much, if not more in my own interest, than from any love of or desire to help Meighen. . . .'[42]

That disagreement, while over and done with, was perhaps never quite forgotten and the following weeks brought further aggravations to Mackenzie King over Byng's conduct towards him. They were seemingly little things but in King's mind they had a large and sinister significance. One night he took some dinner guests to a hockey game, Lady Byng having asked him to lend the event his patronage. When he got there the Byngs did not treat him with very great respect. 'I spoke to Their Excellencies during the first and second intermission,' runs his version of the incident in the diary.

I felt they not only might but should have asked me to come into their box. After all I am the prime minister of the country, and His Ex. is a visiting governor. The fact that at the moment there is a difficult [political] situation only makes me the more indignant that they had not the courtesy to recognize the situation as meriting a little graciousness. The box was full of a lot of people from England who adopt a sort of superior air towards those of us who are in Canada — I confess to a certain feeling of genuine indignation at the action of their excellencies tonight — Toryism.[43]

This shoddy treatment rankled for some time. Three weeks later, having just had 'an unpleasant dream about Govt House' the night before, King encountered Arthur Sladen, the Governor General's principal secretary, whom he regarded as

one of the main Tory influences at Byng's elbow. He told
Sladen that he felt 'distinctly hurt' by the hockey game incident
and he had another grievance for him as well. King had recently
learned that the Governor General's drawing room and the
State dinner, the two big events of the social season, had been
postponed. He seemed to fear that this would be construed, in
view of the uncertain political conditions, as a reflection on the
legitimacy of his Government and of himself as Prime
Minister.[44] Sladen tried to soothe him; the drawing room
would be held the next Saturday as planned and the State
dinner would be put off for a time because Lady Byng had
planned a fancy dress ball to mark her birthday on 11 January,
about the time the dinner would normally be held. But such an
excuse was an additional aggravation to King and he fumed at
'this piece of nonsense', as he called it.[45] 'This is all wrong and
I shall tell His Ex. so if he asks me. Why should a birthday
party precede a state function!'[46] However, he overcame his
pique sufficiently to go along to the party, attired as, of all
things, a courtier in the reign of George III.[47]

As if all this was not enough, King, undertaking to explain to
His Excellency what would probably occur in the early days of
the forthcoming parliamentary session, and affirming that he
had done the right thing in staying in office, detected a distinct
coolness in Byng.

> His Ex. listened and simply said 'Of course, I do not agree'
> — there was nothing gracious in his manner it was that
> Tory air of superior knowledge and station which makes
> a man with red blood in his veins feel a deep resentment. . . .
> I confess I felt as I came away real indignation at an
> attitude which if it means and spells anything means and
> spells 'colonialism' for Canada. Lord Byng had a chance
> to help to end that. . . .[48]

To cap all Mackenzie King's annoyances with Byng, the latter
came to him not long after the session began with a remarkably
naïve and, to King, objectionable proposition. He wanted
authorisation to ask Meighen to consult the Prime Minister
'with a view to our arranging a *modus operandi* for carrying on
the session — a programme in the interest of Canada.'
Evidently Byng was appalled by the bitterness of partisan

strife in the House of Commons and thought that the game then being played there was irrelevant to the real needs of the country. The man on the street, he argued, would be favourably impressed if the two leaders rose above their differences and united for the common good. King gave the idea short shrift, advising the Governor to stay out of it 'and let the situation be solved in the H. of C. not at Rideau Hall. It is the old ctry idea,' wrote King, ' — that he is here to *save Canada*. . . This is really old country interference . . . the point of view that we are incapable of managing our own affairs. With any knowledge of politics Lord Byng would never make a suggestion of this kind.'[49] Arthur Meighen, who could seldom agree with King about anything, would surely have agreed with that last comment, confident as he was that he finally had his despised opponent on the skids.

Mackenzie King, though, became certain that the whole thing was a plot by the Tories to ease themselves into power. One of his followers had been asked by a prominent Conservative MP during a chance meeting on the street why their two leaders didn't get together. Hearing this, King decided that the idea had been hatched by the Tories, put in Lady Byng's ear by R.B. Bennett, 'a great friend of Her Ex.', and in this way transmitted to her husband.[50] Thus did the significance of Byng's not very carefully considered but well meant suggestion become blown up out of all proportions.

All these controversies and vexatious incidents following the 1925 election may have convinced King that he could not now confidently count on Lord Byng to do the 'right thing', that His Excellency was no longer quite the 'dear dear friend' and 'noble companion' King had once thought him to be. At any rate, it is clear that he did not think the dissolution of Parliament he decided to ask for, with his Government facing imminent defeat in the House of Commons on a motion of censure, was his for the asking. He failed to get it, of course, despite his incessant badgering of Byng for three days running, nor was he able to persuade His Excellency that, before making up his mind, he should cable London for advice. One authority on all this has concluded that in rejecting the request for a dissolution, Lord Byng 'made the right decision for the wrong reasons'.[51] That may be; Byng at the moment appears to have had no very clear grasp of the constitutional arguments to support his decision.

At least, however, he had enough common sense, enough feeling for the fitness of things, to turn down the improper advice of a counsellor who claimed to speak with great knowledge of the constitution but whose understanding of the constitutional issues involved was at least as imperfect as his own.

Throughout those few nasty days in the early summer of 1926, and afterwards, Lord Byng comported himself with perfect dignity, refraining in the face of severe provocation from engaging in argument or recrimination. He agreed to a short extension of his term so that he could install whatever government resulted from the election in September, which became necessary when the administration formed by Meighen after King's resignation itself was defeated in the House. The victor in the election was Mackenzie King and one imagines that the installation of his new Government was a ceremony fraught with some emotion. Having performed it, Baron Byng of Vimy sailed away home to become a Viscount and, later, Commissioner of the Metropolitan Police. Upon accepting that position, one probably better suited to his training and experience than the Governor Generalship of Canada, he wrote to his friend Buchan: 'How the shades of my two ancestors Thomas Wentworth (Earl of Strafford), and Admiral Byng must be chuckling to see me following their footsteps to the scaffold and the quarter deck.'[52] But in some ways, one would think, his work as Commissioner must have seemed simple and straightforward compared to what he had recently gone through as His Majesty's representative in the senior dominion.

NOTES

1. Queen's University Archives, John Buchan Papers, Byng to Buchan, 20 September 1921.
2. Eugene A. Forsey, *The Royal Power of Dissolution of Parliament in the British Commonwealth* (Toronto, 1943, 1968) supersedes all earlier scholarly treatments of the constitutional questions involved and has not been successfully challenged since its publication. The story is told from the perspective of the chief political antagonists in H. Blair Neatby, *William Lyon Mackenzie King, 1924-32: The Lonely Heights* (Toronto, 1963) and Roger Graham *Arthur Meighen a Biography: And Fortune Fled, 1920-27* (Toronto, 1963). A selection of documents and commentaries will be found in Roger Graham (ed.), *The King-Byng Affair: A Question of Responsible Government* (Toronto, 1967).
3. J.R. Mallory, 'The Appointment of the Governor General: Responsib Government, Autonomy, and the Royal Prerogative,' *Canadian Journal of Economics and Political Science*, vol. XXVI, No. 1 (Feb. 1960), pp.98-9.
4. Graham, *Arthur Meighen*, pp.108-9.
5. H. Willis-O'Connor, as told to Madge MacBeth, *Inside Government House* (Toronto, 1954), p.11.
6. Queen's Unviersity Archives, Mackenzie King Diary (microfiche copy of typed transcript), 12 Aug. 1921.
7. Ibid., 31 Jan. 1922.
8. Ibid., 23 Feb. 1922.
9. Ibid., 10 Nov. 1924.
10. Willis-O'Connor, op. cit., p.21.
11. J. Castell Hopkins, *Canadian Annual Review of Public Affairs, 1921* (Toronto, 1922), p.249.
12. King Diary, 17 April 1926.
13. J.E. Esberey, 'A New Look at the King-Byng Dispute,' *Canadian Journal of Political Science*, VI, 1, pp.37-55.
14. King Diary, 11 April 1926.
15. Ibid., 12 Aug. 1921.
16. Ibid., 1 Jan. 1922; 21 Oct. 1922; 31 Dec. 1922; 19 Jan. 1924; 3 Nov. 1925; 17 Feb. 1924; 30 Oct. 1925.
17. Ibid., 2 Sept. 1921.
18. Ibid., 28 June 1926.
19. Buchan Papers, Lady Byng to Buchan, 21 July [1926], private.
20. King Diary, 2 Sept. 1921.
21. R. MacGregor Dawson, *William Lyon Mackenzie King, a Political Biography, 1874-1923* (Toronto, 1958), p.374.
22. King Diary, 8 Nov. 1925.
23. Ibid., 12 Aug. 1921.
24. Ibid., 11 March 1923.
25. Ibid., 3 Feb. 1922.
26. Ibid., 10 Nov. 1924.
27. Ibid., 20 Sept. 1924.

28. Ibid., 21 Oct. 1922.
29. Ibid., 24 Feb. 1924.
30. Ibid., 23 Nov. 1924.
31. Ibid., 19 Jan. 1924.
32. Ibid., 26 Jan. 1924.
33. Ibid., 21 Jan. 1925.
34. Ibid., 22 Feb. 1925.
35. Ibid., 29 March 1925.
36. Ibid., 4 Sept. 1925.
37. Ibid., 13 Sept. 1925.
38. Buchan Papers, Byng to Buchan, 12 May 1925, private.
39. Ibid., Byng to Buchan, 24 Oct. 1925.
40. King Diary, 4 Sept. 1925.
41. Ibid., 30 Oct. 1925.
42. Ibid., 3 Nov. 1925.
43. Ibid., 19 Nov. 1925.
44. Ibid., 21 Nov. 1925.
45. Ibid., 4 Dec. 1925.
46. Ibid., 8 Dec. 1925.
47. Ibid., 11 Jan. 1925.
48. Ibid., 30 Nov. 1925.
49. Ibid., 24 Jan. 1926.
50. Ibid., 17 Feb. 1926.
51. Neatby, op. cit., p. 149.
52. Buchan Papers, Byng to Byng to Buchan, 22 June 1928.

Dwight David Eisenhower

STEPHEN AMBROSE

Dwight David Eisenhower was the only professional soldier to live in the White House in the twentieth century. He was also the only Cold War President who did not get the US involved in a shooting war, and this despite the high tensions of the 1950s, tensions that offered him numerous opportunities to wave the flag and start the shooting. Eisenhower was elected, in part, because of his promise to end a war, and he did end it within four months of taking office. On an average annual basis, he spent the least amount of money on the armed services of all America's Cold War Presidents. He believed that the purpose of armed forces was to protect a way of life. What he most feared, next to a nuclear disaster, was that the Cold War would force the US to follow the eighteenth-century Prussian example, where the nation existed in order to serve the army, and in addition drive the United States into bankruptcy.

Eisenhower's hatred of Communism knew almost no bounds. He wanted desperately to stop what he called the Red Tide from taking over South-East Asia — he coined the 'falling dominoes' phrase — but not desperately enough to rip apart the fabric of the American system or to endanger peace. When Eisenhower took office the Korean War was still raging. The right-wingers in his own party, led by Senators like Styles Bridges, Joseph R. McCarthy and William Knowland, supported by Vice-President Richard Nixon, were crying 'Back to the Mainland'. They wanted Chiang Kai-shek 'unleashed' and atomic bombs dropped on China. Eisenhower gave the China lobby a stern rebuke in his first major foreign policy address on 16 April 1953, before the American Society of Newspaper Editors.

The President spoke on 'The Chance for Peace', and in the speech he set the theme for his eight years as Chief Executive.

113

'Every gun that is fired, every war ship launched,' he declared, 'signified in the final sense, a theft from those who hunger and are not fed. . . . The cost of one modern heavy bomber is this: a modern brick school in more than thirty cities. . . .' After giving additional examples of the domestic cost of the garrison state that would be required to carry on a military crusade against Communism, Eisenhower stated flatly, 'This is not a way of life at all.' He was a true conservative.

Eisenhower was the last President to be born in the nineteenth century. He had the nineteenth-century American's abhorrence of a standing army, and a nineteenth-century commitment to the idea that the US ought to serve as an example, rather than as a policeman, to the rest of the world. Further, as a professional soldier he knew the *limits* of military power, as well as the cost. He was genuinely frightened of big government and realised that nothing made government bigger, or gave it more control over the private lives of its citizens, than constant involvement in foreign wars. He was also an old-fashioned Republican who believed in the necessity of a balanced budget. As with his Republican successors, that meant reductions in domestic spending on welfare programmes. Unlike his successors, Eisenhower knew that the real culprit of the unbalanced budget was the Department of Defense, and he made extensive cuts there too.

All of which may sound simple-minded, but as Murray Kempton reminds us, Eisenhower was 'the great tortoise upon whose back the world sat for eight years. We laughed at him; we talked wistfully about moving; and all the while we never knew the cunning beneath the shell.' Or as Don Whitehead put it in an article on Normandy, 'Eisenhower was a far more complicated man than he seemed to be — a man who shaped events with such subtlety that he left others thinking they were the architects of those events. And he was satisfied to leave it that way.'

He was indeed. In my view his greatest contribution as a soldier was his grand strategy — I rate him as an equal to the best strategists the US has produced — but that point can be, has been, and will be debated. What is not debatable was his ability to lead an alliance. Even such bitter critics as Field Marshal Bernard Law Montgomery and Lord Alanbrooke have agreed that Eisenhower's special triumph was to see to it that the Allies not only won the war, but that they won it as Allies. He was a master at seeking compromise, or — when compromise was impossible — at making sure everyone had a chance to have his say before announcing his decision. His low-key approach, even in his lofty position of Supreme Commander, Allied Expeditionary Force, was to convince, not order, and he gave his subordinates considerable lee-way. But as Montgomery could testify, when the time came Eisenhower could be firm enough.

Eisenhower had a highly sophisticated approach to the political problems inherent in an alliance command, of which the most important part was his insistence, always, that he was a simple soldier operating only on the basis of military criteria. That sounds like a contradiction, perhaps, but I don't think it is. Eisenhower instinctively knew that if he ever admitted that he was making decisions on political grounds, the alliance would weaken. It was perfectly obvious to him that the British — not to mention the Russians — had a different set of war aims than the Americans. The only thing holding the strange alliance together was the common enemy; Eisenhower knew that he had to make his British and Canadian subordinates believe that he was making his decisions solely on the grounds of what would bring about the swiftest Nazi defeat. But he was by no means so naïve as to believe that himself; he knew perfectly well that political factors had to play a major role in his strategy. His job was to keep those political factors out of sight, and for the most part he was successful in doing so. Two examples may illustrate the point.

In September 1944, Montgomery demanded that Eisenhower stop the Americans under General George Patton in the vicinity of Paris, put General Courtney Hodges' Army under British command, give all incoming supplies to the 21st Army Group (under Montgomery's command), and then turn 21st Army Group loose for a single thrust into Berlin. Eishenhower refused, primarily on the grounds of military and logistical factors, but also because he was concerned with political factors begond Montgomery's scope.

National feelings in England and the US had been inflamed during the battle for Normandy. The Americans were getting cocky as a result of General Omar Bradley's breakout and Patton's rapid advances. In personal encounters, in the press, and on the radio, they tended to make cutting remarks about Montgomery's lack of action before Caen. The British were resentful and tried to counter by emphasising Montgomery's earlier role as over-all ground commander. Both sides were beginning to brag about the accomplishments of their own armies while ignoring or minimising the activities of their partners. Eisenhower pleaded with reporters to write about 'Allied' advances instead of British or American or Canadian victories, but with little success. If in this situation he had stopped Patton and put Hodges under Montgomery, there would have been an enormous outcry in the American press.

In addition, American divisions were piling up, waiting to enter the battle. Eisenhower needed a broad front on which to deploy them. If he had not used them, the War Department would have been hard pressed to justify the decision to raise and train them. Another political pressure came from the French, who wanted to liberate those parts of their country still occupied by the Germans.

Political pressures cannot be overemphasised, notwith-standing Eisenhower's oft-repeated declaration that he made his decisions on military grounds alone. The truth of the matter is that there never was more than the slimmest chance that Montgomery would be able to persuade Eisenhower to stop Patton where he was and put Hodges under a British commander. No matter how brilliant or logical Montgomery's plan for an advance to the Ruhr, and no matter what the nature of Montgomery's personality, under no circumstances would Eisenhower willingly have given all the glory to the British. The American people would not have stood for it, nor would Patton, Bradley, Chief of Staff George C. Marshall, or President Franklin Roosevelt. Had the troops of the Allied Expeditionary Force been composed of only one nationality, Eisenhower might have adopted some version of Montgomery's plan. The Supreme Commander almost never admitted that the alliance created problems on the battlefront, but once, in Italy, he confessed in a private memorandum, 'I think we have made Allied command work here with reasonable efficiency, even though at times it lacks the drive that could be applied were the force entirely homogeneous with respect to nationality.' As things stood, however, Eisenhower could not make his decisions solely on military grounds. He could not halt Patton in his tracks, relegate Bradley to a minor administrative role, and in effect tell Marshall that the great army he had raised in the United States was not needed in Europe.

The Combined Chiefs of Staff never entered the dispute, for it was not a matter for their intervention. The alternatives arose from a plan of campaign whose object and shape they had already set and involved forces already within the theatre. They were not called upon to provide reinforcements to support either the single thrust or the broad front; indeed, they had already provided more troops than Eisenhower could use. The individual members of the CCS followed the argument closely but did not interfere.

Although it seemed that Eisenhower was the only one who recognised the political requirements and made the necessary adjustments, this was only a result of the organisational set-up. Allanbrooke and Marshall had to argue for their own national forces, and it was Bradley's and Montgomery's responsibility to urge on Eisenhower their best military advice. It was Eisenhower's duty to see the situation as a whole. Had the disagreement come before the CCS as a body, however, it is likely the Chiefs would have made the same decision as Eisenhower, on the same grounds, with the emphasis on political necessity. Like Eisenhower, their ultimate responsibility was to the alliance.

The second example of Eisenhower's need to make political choices revolves around the last decision of the war. By March 1945, victory was imminent. Every alliance in history has broken up once victory was achieved, but Roosevelt hoped to hold this one together, primarily through the device of the United Nations, just then being formed./The President thought it important for the US to make every effort to get along with the Russians, for in his view post-war cooperation between the US and the USSR was essential to world peace. Prime Minister Winston Churchill, however, believed that once Hitler had been defeated there was no basis for British-American cooperation with Russia; he was more concerned with building the strength of the Western Allies in Central Europe as a buffer against Communism than he was in getting along with Stalin.

There was also the question of glory. Each member of the Big Three felt that it had made the major contribution to the war effort and ought to receive the credit for the final triumph. Each could make a good argument: the Russians had defeated the bulk of the German Army; the British had fought alone against Hitler in 1940-41; the US had supplied much of the military material for the other partners in the alliance. The truth was that all three nations were essential to the victory; none could have done it alone or even in an alliance with only one other nation. Yet each nation wanted credit for the victory. In the last days of the war, this came down to one thing — each wanted its army to be the first to take Berlin.

The desire of all three nations to be the first into Berlin brought about some of Eisenhower's most difficult moments in the war. He had to decide, first, whether or not to race his forces against the Red Army to Berlin, and second, if he did start a race for the capital, whether to send British or American divisions. Whatever he did would make two nations unhappy.

Patton wanted Eisenhower to hold Montgomery's forces on the Rhine and give him their supplies so that he, Patton, could dash on to Berlin. Montgomery wanted Patton stopped where he was, with all Patton's supplies sent to 21st Army Group, so that Montgomery could send the British into Berlin. Churchill hoped that British troops would take the city, but he was mostly concerned with getting Western troops there before the Russians. Roosevelt was opposed to any race for Berlin.

Eisenhower decided to leave Berlin to the Red Army and instead directed his forces toward what was left of the German Army, mainly in the south. His decision has become one of the most controversial of the war. His critics charge that he did not understand international politics — that by leaving Berlin to the Russians he lost the best chance the West had to prevent Communist control of Berlin and the surrounding territory of East Germany. The critics believe that had Eisenhower taken Berlin, the Russians could have been kept out of the city and their post-war territorial gains in Eastern Europe minimised.

The critics are badly mistaken, their charges absurd. There was never the slightest chance that the Russians could have been forced out of Eastern Europe, which the Red Army had liberated while the Western Allies were still on the west bank of the Rhine River. Nothing could have driven the Russians out of the territory they had already conquered. Beyond that, the division of Germany into occupation zones had already been made at the Yalta Conference. No matter who captured Berlin, the politicians had already agreed to split the city into sectors, with each nation getting a part of Berlin. There is no reason to believe that if the Western Allies had captured Berlin they would have gone back on their word and kept the Russians out. In short, in terms of the politics of the post-war world, it made no difference who captured Berlin. Also, Eisenhower was told by Bradley that it would cost 100,000 casualties to take Berlin, a stiff price for prestige. And holding down losses among citizen soldiers is, after all, a political decision.

In early April 1945, when the Allied armies were across the Rhine River and sweeping through Germany, Churchill nevertheless put extreme pressure on Eisenhower to drive to Berlin. Eisenhower replied that it made no military sense to strike out for Berlin, because 'Berlin itself is no longer a particularly important objective. Its usefullness to the Germans has been largely destroyed and even his government is preparing to move to another area.' Moreover, Eisenhower realised what no one else seemed to, namely, that by concentrating on destroying the Wehrmacht rather than on getting to Berlin first or on keeping the Russians out of Central Europe, he could hold the alliance together, at least until Hitler's defeat was complete. While everyone around him argued for his own nation's aims, Eisenhower stuck to the needs of the alliance.

Eisenhower was always clear about his goal. His orders from the CCS were to defeat Germany — not to stop the Russian advance or to make sure Montgomery got to Berlin. 'I am the first to admit that a war is waged in pursuance of political aims,' Eisenhower told Churchill, 'and if the CCS should decide that the Allied effort to take Berlin outweighs purely military considerations in this theater, I would cheerfully readjust my plans and my thinking so as to carry out such an operation.' Thus, if Churchill was prepared to declare Russia the enemy instead of Germany and could get Roosevelt to agree, Eisenhower would willingly change his plans, for then the military considerations would be much different. But the CCS did not change his orders and the final decision stayed in his hands. Germany remained the enemy; Russia continued to be an ally. Despite some stupid talk from Patton about linking up with the Wehrmacht to drive the Red Army back to the Volga, Eisenhower knew that the best hope for the world was

Big Three cooperation after the war.

In late April 1945 the Russians battered their way into Berlin, where at a cost of 100,000 casualties they gained the first sombre sense of triumph, the first awesome sight of the ruins, the first parades under the pall of smoke. Two months later they gave up to the West — as previously agreed — over half the city they had captured at such an enormous price. At the cost of not a single life, Britain and the US had their sectors in Berlin. They have been there ever since.

The Big Three broke up anyway — although it was most certainly not Eisenhower's fault — and the Cold War ensued. Eisenhower, as President, had to deal with it. He did so on the same basis he had fought in the war — hold down the casualties, hold down the cost, do your best to compromise, and hold on to your friends. He worked within a framework of extreme hatred of Communism, however, and he was not above taking political advantage of the American people's desire to 'do something' about Communist enslavement of Eastern Europe, thereby raising false hopes and expectations.

'We can never rest', Eisenhower said during his 1952 Presidential campaign, 'until the enslaved nations of the world have in the fullness of freedom the right to choose their own path, for then, and then only, can we say that there is a possible way of living peacefully and permanently with Communism in the world.' Like most campaign statements, Eisenhower's bowed to both sides of the political spectrum. For the bold he indicated a policy of liberation, while the cautious could take comfort in his willingness to someday live peacefully with the Communists. Since the Americans believed, however, that no one could freely choose Communism, Eisenhower's statement had a major internal contradiction.

In practice, despite the promises of liberation in the Republican platform, Eisenhower and Secretary of State John Foster Dulles continued President Harry S. Truman's policy of containment. There was no basic difference between their foreign policy and that of their predecessors, which they had strongly denounced, but they avoided embarrassment over their lack of action through their rhetoric. 'We can never rest,' Eisenhower had said, but rest they did, except in their speeches.

Those speeches helped hide the fact that they did nothing to liberate the enslaved, but perhaps more important to their popularity was their unwillingness to risk American lives, for here too they were expressing the deep sentiments of their countrymen. On occasion Eisenhower rattled the sabre and filled the air with denunciations of the Communists, but he also shut down the Korean War and reduced the size of the armed forces. Despite intense pressure and great temptation, he entered no wars. He was willing to supply material, on a limited scale, to others so that they could fight the enemy, but he would not commit American boys to the struggle. Like Truman he did his best to contain Communism; unlike Truman he did not use American troops to do so. His speeches provided emotional satisfaction but his actions failed to liberate a single slave. No one had the right to complain that the Republicans had been misleading, however, for the policy had been clearly spelled out in the campaign. The vague and militant talk about liberation was balanced by specific promises to end the war in Korea — without liberating North Korea, much less China — and to balance the budget.

The extent of the commitment to fiscal soundness was best seen in the New Look, the term Eisenhower coined to describe his military policy. It combined domestic, military and foreign considerations. The New Look rejected the premise of the Truman Administration that the US could spend up to 20 per cent of its GNP on arms; it rejected deficit financing; it maintained that enough rearmament had been accomplished to provide security for the US and to support a policy of containment.

The New Look became fixed policy during a period of lessened tensions and American military superiority, but it did not depend on either for its continuation. In its eight years of power, the Eisenhower Administration went through a series of war scares and it witnessed the development of Soviet long-range bombers, ballistic missiles and nuclear weapons. Throughout, however, Eisenhower held to the New Look. His Defense Department expenditures remained in the $35 to $40 billion range.

In 1956, when the Soviets had nearly caught up with the American Armed Services, the Eisenhower Administration subjected the New Look to careful scrutiny. Three alternatives were examined. Admiral Arthur W. Radford, Chairman of the

Joint Chiefs of Staff, proposed to continue the existing level of military spending but to maintain a clear superiority in nuclear forces by making major cutbacks in conventional strength. He wanted to begin by cutting the Army by nearly half a million men. The Democrats in Congress went beyond Radford's proposal. They insisted on maintaining conventional strength at current levels while increasing Air Force appropriations by nearly $1 billion. Eisenhower, typically, chose a third course. Like Radford, he wanted to stabilise military expenditure; like the Senate Democrats he was opposed to reducing conventional forces. He disagreed with both on the fundamental question — should the US maintain superiority? Eisenhower's answer was no. For him sufficiency was enough. He refused either to reduce the Army or to increase the Air Force. In fact, America retained superiority, but only because the Soviets did not increase their armament as rapidly as expected.

The key to the New Look was the American ability to build and deliver nuclear weapons. Put more bluntly, Eisenhower's military policy rested on America's capacity to destroy the Soviet Union. Soviet strides in military technology gave them the ability to retaliate, but not to defend Russia, which was the major reason Eisenhower could accept sufficiency. The US did not have to be superior to the Soviet Union to be able to demolish it.

To give up superiority was not easy, however, and it rankled with many Americans, especially in the military. Eisenhower had his greatest difficulties with the Army, for it suffered most from his refusal to increase the Defense Department budget. Three Army Chiefs of Staff resigned in protest and one of them, General Maxwell Taylor, later became the chief adviser on military affairs to Eisenhower's successor and saw his views triumph. The Army wanted enough flexibility to be able to meet the Communist threat at any level. The trouble with Eisenhower's New Look, the Army Chiefs and some Democrats argued, was that it locked the US into an all-or-nothing response. Wherever and whenever conflict broke out, the Chiefs wanted to be capable of moving in. To do so, they needed a huge standing army, with specialised divisions, elite groups, a wide variety of weapons, and an enormous transportation capacity.

Eisenhower insisted that the cost of being able to intervene anywhere, immediately, was unbearable. 'Let us not forget', the

President wrote a friend in August of 1956, 'that the Armed Services are to defend a "way of life," not merely land, property or lives.' He wanted to make the Chiefs accept the need for a 'balance between minimum requirements in the costly implements of war and the health of our economy.'

The New Look meant that Eisenhower had abandoned his former advocacy of universal military training, with its assumption that the next war would resemble World War II. More fundamentally, he had abandoned the idea of America fighting any more Korean wars. \Eisenhower's policy emphasised both the importance of tactical nuclear weapons and the role of strategic air power as a deterrent to aggression. He used technology to mediate between conflicting political goals. Big bombers carrying nuclear weapons were the means through which he reconciled lower military expenditures with a foreign policy of containment.

The New Look shaped foreign policy. Since it was almost his only weapon, Dulles had to flash a nuclear bomb whenever he wanted to threaten the use of force. To make the threat believable, the US developed smaller atomic weapons that could be used tactically on the battlefield. Dulles then attempted to convince the world that the US would not hesitate to use them. The fact that the NATO forces were so small made the threat persuasive, for there was no other way to stop the Red Army in Europe. Both Dulles and Eisenhower made this explicit. Eisenhower declared, 'Where these things are used on strictly military targets . . . I see no reason why they shouldn't be used just exactly as you would use a bullet or anything else.'

The administration used massive retaliation, or the threat of it, as its chief instrument of containment. In 1956 Dulles called the overall method brinkmanship, which he explained in an article in *Life* magazine. 'You have to take chances for peace, just as you must take chances in war. Of course we were brought to the verge of war. The ability to get to the verge without getting into the war is the necessary art. . . . If you try to run away from it, if you are scared to go to the brink, you are lost. We've had to look it square in the face. . . . We walked to the brink and we looked it in the face. We took strong action.'

Eisenhower and Dulles implicitly recognised the limitations on brinkmanship. They never tried to use it for liberation and they used it much more sparingly after the Soviets were able to threaten the US itself with destruction. It was a tactic to support containment at an acceptable cost, within a limited time span under a specific set of military circumstances, not a strategy for protracted conflict.

In his *Life* article, Dulles cited instances of going to the brink. The first was in Korea. When Eisenhower took office, the truce talks were stalled on the question of prisoner of war repatriation. The Chinese wanted all their men held by the UN command returned, while the Americans insisted on voluntary repatriation. The talks, and the war, continued. The Chinese would not give.

During the campaign, Eisenhower had promised to bring about peace in Korea. Emmet John Hughes reports that he was enthusiastic about the General's commitment to peace, but felt an 'unhappy need' to remind Eisenhower of how far removed Dulles' views were from Eisenhower's. Dulles had just told Hughes that it would not serve America's purpose if the Communists accepted a compromise in Korea because the US could not 'get much out of a Korean settlement until we have shown — before all Asia — our clear superiority by giving the Chinese one hell of a licking.' When Eisenhower heard this, 'He stood very still for an instant, then he snapped out the words: "All right, then. If Mr. Dulles and all his sophisticated advisers really mean that they can *not* talk peace seriously, then I am in the wrong pew. For if it's *war* we should be talking about, I know the people to give me advice on that — and they're not in the State Department. Now either we cut out this fooling around and make a serious bid for peace — or we forget the whole thing." '

After his election, but before his inauguration, Eisenhower made a trip to Korea. General Mark Clark, in command in Korea, presented him with a 'detailed estimate of the forces and plans required to obtain a military victory.' Eisenhower never even looked at them. Clark realised that the President-elect was determined to 'seek an honourable truce'. Eisenhower's visit persuaded the President-elect that involvement in a land war in Asia was a disaster for America.

Eisenhower returned to the US on 14 December 1952, determined to cut losses and get out. He warned that unless the war ended quickly, the US might strike at China 'under circumstances of our own choosing'. Armistice talks, which had broken down, recommenced in April 1953, but again there was no progress on the POW question. Dulles then warned Peking, through India, that if peace did not come the US would bring in atomic weapons. Eleven days later the two sides agreed to place the question of prisoner repatriation in the hands of international, neutral authorities. Although Dr. Syngman Rhee tried to upset the arrangements, in late July a military armistice was signed. The Korean War was over; brinkmanship had achieved its goal.

But there were limits to what brinkmanship could accomplish, as seen a year later when Eisenhower had an opportunity to initiate a bold new foreign policy. In the spring of 1954, as the French position at Dien Bien Phu in north-western Vietnam steadily got worse, Eisenhower was subjected to pressure to save the French. Vice-President Nixon said, on 16 April 1954, that 'if to avoid further Communist expansion in Asia and Indochina, we must take the risk now by putting our boys in. I think the Executive has to take the politically unpopular decision and do it.' Dulles heartily agreed. Air Force Chief of Staff Nathan Twining wanted to drop three small atomic bombs on the Vietminh around Dien Bien Phu, 'and clean those Commies out of there.' The Chairman of the Joint Chiefs, Admiral Radford, said he had aircraft carriers in the area and was anxious to intervene. Only Army Chief of Staff Matthew Ridgway was opposed; he feared that America would get tied down in an endless war on the Asian mainland.

Eisenhower was anxious to do something — he had promised liberation but had failed to bring it about anywhere — and now Vietnam was on the verge of falling to the Communists. He could envision Democrats gleefully demanding to know 'Who Lost Vietnam?' The temptation to launch an executive war, as Truman had done in Korea, was great, but Eisenhower's 'fundamental concept of the Presidency', as he put it, 'is that we have a constitutional government,' which required Congressional action before committing American troops to combat. Consequently, Eisenhower insisted on three conditions before intervening in Vietnam. First, the French must promise full independence to all Vietnam, so that Ho Chi Minh could not claim that he was fighting a war of national liberation. Second, the British had to agree to give active support. Eisenhower believed that without a coalition to provide 'real moral standing', intervention could easily be seen as a 'brutal example of imperialism'. This was particularly true, he wrote, because there was no evidence of Chinese participation in the war. Third, Congress had to provide positive support, perhaps even in the form of a declaration of war.

None of the conditions were met, as I suspect Eisenhower knew in advance they would not be. The adventuristic Asia-firsters in the Republican Party, and the hawks among the military, were surprised and disappointed at the general absence of enthusiasm among Congressmen for American involvement in another Asian war. In effect, Eisenhower had told the hawks to convince Congress, not the President, to march off on a crusade, and that proved to be an impossible task.

Eisenhower successfully avoided the trap of Vietnam partly because of his fear of the cost, partly because of his own blend of military and political wisdom. For, like Ridgway, Eisenhower knew in advance the hopelessness of the military situation. he had told the French, even before they committed 10,000 crack troops to Dien Bien Phu, that it was a mistake. Eisenhower said that any good soldier knew 'the almost invariable fate of troops invested in an isolated fortress' that could be supplied only by air. He also realised that the racist and colonial nature of the war made it difficult at best for the French (or the Americans) to impose a military solution. Like Charles De Gaulle, Eisenhower seems to have realised that the era of the white man in Asia was over. There is an irony here — two professional soldiers, serving as heads of government, realised the limitations of military power in a way that their political counterparts never did. Both Eisenhower and De Gaulle were far too wise to believe that there was a military solution to a political problem like Vietnam.

Nor did Eisenhower believe that bloated military budgets were the way to keep the economy booming. When in late 1958 Soviet Premier Nikita Khrushchev threatened to write a peace treaty with East Germany and turn control of access to Berlin over to the East Germans. Eisenhower was under intense pressure from the Democrats and the military to increase America's Armed Services dramatically as a prelude to taking a hard line with Khrushchev over Berlin. Eisenhower pointed out that 'this would solve any unemployment problem but it would also make certain that we become a garrison state.' In March 1959, as Khrushchev's deadline approached, and the Pentagon prepared plans for mobilisation, Eisenhower told Congress that he did not need additional money for missiles or conventional warfare forces to deal with the crisis.

At a press conference on 11 March, he was asked if the US was prepared to 'use nuclear war to defend free Berlin?' Eisenhower replied, 'Well, I don't know how you could free anything with nuclear weapons.' Peter Lisagor of the Chicago *Daily News* then asked if there was 'an in-between response.' Eisenhower fixed Lisagor with a stare and declared, 'I think we might as well understand this — might as well all of us understand this: destruction is not a good police force. You don't throw hand grenades around streets to police the streets so that people won't be molested by thugs.' Another reporter referred to the Pentagon's advocacy of mobilisation and beefing up the forces in Germany. Eisenhower responded with a question of his own: What in heaven's name would the US do with more ground forces in Europe? Thumping the table, he declared, 'We are certainly not going to fight a ground war in Europe,' and pointed out the elementary truth that a few more men or even a few more divisions in Europe would have no real effect on the military balance there. He said the greatest danger in the Berlin crisis was that the Russians would frighten the US into an arms race that would bankrupt the country. A few months later, when Khrushchev was visiting Eisenhower at Camp David, Khrushchev denied that he had set a time limit, and the crisis was past.

Two years later, by way of contrast, President John F. Kennedy faced a similar threat. Kennedy received the same advice Eisenhower had received, but the new President took it. Kennedy put a $3.2 billion additional military budget through Congress, tripled the draft calls, extended enlistments, and mobilised 158,000 Reserves and National Guardsmen. Altogether he increased the size of the armed forces by 300,000 men, sending 40,000 of them to Europe. In the upshot, the results were the same — Khrushchev backed down.

Eisenhower displayed his moderation and caution throughout his administration, during the Hungarian-Suez crisis of 1956, for example, or in his stationing of troops in Lebanon in 1958, or in the Quemoy-Matsu crises of 1955 and 1958. Nor did he panic in response to Sputnik and the supposed bomber gap and missile gap. Again the pressure was on him to 'do something', to 'get the country moving again', especially when in late 1957 the newspapers discovered and published the findings and recommendations of a blue-ribbon committee headed by H. Rowan Gaither, Jr., of the Ford Foundation, which painted an exceedingly dark picture of the future of American security. The Gaither Report, as Eisenhower typically understated it, included 'some sobering observations'. It found that the Soviet GNP was increasing at a much faster rate than that of the US, that the Russians were spending as much on their armed forces and heavy industry as the Americans were, that the Soviets had enough fissionable material for 1,500 nuclear weapons, with 4,500 jet bombers, 300 long-range submarines and an extensive air defence system, that they had been producing ballistic missiles with a 700-mile range, that by 1959 the Soviets might be able to launch an attack against the US with 100 ICBMs carrying megaton-sized nuclear warheads, and that if such an attack should come the civilian population and the American bombers in SAC would be vulnerable.

The Gaither Report recommended a much improved defence. The committee wanted fall-out shelters built on a massive scale, an improvement of America's air defence capability, a vast increase in SAC's offensive power, a build-up of conventional forces capable of fighting limited war, and another reorganisation of the Pentagon. As a starter, the Gaither Report (and a somewhat similar study done by the Rockefeller Foundation) urged an increase in defence spending to $48 billion.

Eisenhower said no. 'We could not turn the nation into a garrison state,' he explained in his memoirs, adding as an afterthought that the Gaither Report was 'useful; it acted as a gadfly.' He kept the defence budget under $40 billion, quietly rejected the demands for fall-out shelters and increased conventional war capability, and dropped one Army division and a number of tactical air wings from active duty. He did disperse SAC bombers and he speeded up the ballistic missile programmes, although Congress had to appropriate more funds than the administration requested for the ICBM and Polaris programmes to get them into high gear.

Democrats charged that the Republicans were allowing their Neanderthal fiscal views to endanger the national security, but Eisenhower knew what he was doing. The CIA, in one of the great intelligence *coups* of all time, had in 1956 inaugurated a series of flights over the Soviet Union in high altitude aeroplanes, called U-2s. The photographs that resulted from the flights revealed, as Eisenhower later put it, 'proof that the horrors of the alleged "bomber gap" and the later "missile gap" were nothing more than imaginative creations of irresponsibility.' The US still had a substantial lead in strategic weapons.

One of the most important points about the U-2 flights was that Khrushchev knew they were taking place, which meant that Khrushchev knew that Eisenhower knew how hollow were the Soviet boasts about strategic superiority. The fact that Eisenhower made no strong statements about Soviet inferiority during the American domestic controversy about the missile gap tended to reassure the Soviets and convince them that the President really was a man of moderation who was sincerely interested in some sort of *modus vivendi*. The flights, the information they produced, and Eisenhower's rejection of the Gaither Report, all indicated to the Soviets that Eisenhower had accepted the fundamental idea that neither side could win a nuclear war and that both would lose in an arms race.

The events in the year following Sputnik had the effect of establishing ground rules for the Cold War. By staying out of the Lebanon situation the Soviets indicated that they recognised and would not challenge the West's vital interests. By refusing to take the easy way out of the missile gap controversy, Eisenhower indicated that he did not want an arms race and that he was eager to establish a *modus vivendi*. Through their negative signals, both sides showed that they would keep the threshold of conflict low. The years of Eisenhower's second term marked the height of bipolarity, for as the British, French, Israelis and Egyptians could testify, what the Big Two wanted, they got, at least during a crisis.

Eisenhower and Khrushchev were anxious to solidify the concept of peaceful coexistence, each for his own reasons, but by 1959 the Cold War had gone on for so long that calling it off was no easy task. Both men had to fend off hard-liners at home, both had troubles with their allies, and both were beset by Third World problems that they could neither understand nor control. Eisenhower had trouble with the Democrats, who were unhampered by orthodox fiscal views and who did want an arms race. In their view, government spending would help, not hurt, the economy. The Democrats, led by Senators John F. Kennedy, Lyndon B. Johnson, and Hubert H. Humphrey, were impatient with Eisenhower's conservatism, yearned for a dynamic President and talked incessantly about America's loss of prestige. They wanted to restore America to world leadership, which in practice meant extending American commitments and increasing American arms. On the other side, Eisenhower was beset by Republicans who wanted to hear more about liberation and getting tough with the Communists, and the President himself had by no means escaped from the patterns of thought of the Cold War.

Neither had Khrushchev, who also had hard-liners in Moscow pushing him towards the brink. In addition, Mao had become as much a problem for Khrushchev as Chiang was for Eisenhower. Khrushchev's refusal to support Mao's call for wars of national liberation, one of the causes of the Sino-Russian split, signified to Mao that the Russians had joined the have powers against the have-nots. There was other evidence, such as Khrushchev's trip to the US, his willingness to go to the Geneva summit again, and the cooling of the Berlin crisis. As the Chinese saw it, the Soviets were selling out both Communism and the Third World. They accused Khrushchev of appeasement. Mao's propaganda increasingly warned of winds blowing from the east instead of the west, and of a world-wide revolt of the rural peoples against the urbanites, among whom the Chinese counted the Russians. Mao's radicalism, heightened by his emphasis on racism, appealed strongly to the Third World and made it almost as difficult for the Soviets to influence development in South-East Asia and Africa as it was for the US. Mao challenged, directly and successfully, Khrushchev's leadership of the Communist world. Indirectly, he challenged bipolarity. The world was simply too large, with too much diversity, to be controlled by the two superpowers, no matter how closely together they marched (Mao would soon discover, in Africa, that the world could not be controlled by three powers either).

Khrushchev and Eisenhower had gone too far towards coexistence for the Cold Warriors in their own countries and for their allies. Khrushchev was in the weaker position at home, since Eisenhower was almost immune to criticism on military matters, at least to the public at large. When the Air Force and certain Congressmen demanded that one-third of SAC's bombers be airborne at all times, for example, Eisenhower dismissed the proposal as too costly and not necessary. As one Senator, who was an Air Force supporter, put it, 'How the hell can I argue with "Ike" Eisenhower on military matters?' Khrushchev did not have such prestige and he found it increasingly difficult to ward off those in the Kremlin who wanted more arms and something done about Berlin. He also had to face the Chinese challenge for Communist leadership.

Khrushchev badly needed a Cold War victory, for internal political reasons and to compete with China for followers. He may have felt that Eisenhower, who would shortly be leaving office and who had no pressing need for a resounding personal triumph, would be willing to allow him a victory. Whatever his reasoning, Khrushchev announced on 5 May 1960, on the eve of the Geneva summit meeting, that a Russian surface-to-air missile had knocked down an American U-2 spy plane inside Russia.

The event illustrated more than Khrushchev's flair for the dramatic, for it also showed how entrenched Cold War interests could block any move for peace. Having finally achieved the ability to knock down the U-2s, the Soviets could have waited for the results of the Geneva meeting to actually do it. On the other side, the CIA could have suspended the flights in the period preceding the meeting. Or Khrushchev could have kept quiet about the entire affair, hoping the CIA had learned the lesson and would cease and desist thereafter. Instead, he deliberately embarrassed the President. Khrushchev boasted about the performance of the surface-to-air missiles but concealed the pilot's survival in order to elicit an American explanation that could be demolished by producing the pilot. When Eisenhower fell into the trap, Khrushchev crowed over his discomfort and demanded an apology or a repudiation of Presidential responsibility. He had misjudged the man. Eisenhower stated instead that the US had the right to spy on the Soviet Union and he took full personal responsibility for the flights. The summit conference was ruined. The best hope for an agreement on Berlin was gone.

Khrushchev had improved his position at home, and with the Chinese, but not much. Eisenhower had tried but in the end he was unable to bring the Cold War to a close. Still, despite the U-2 and the wrecked summit meeting, he had improved Russian-American relations. He had failed to liberate any Communist slaves — had indeed been forced to acquiesce in the coming of Communism to Indo-China and Cuba and in the establishment of a Russian base in Egypt — but he had avoided war and kept the arms race at a low level. He had tried, in so far as he was capable, to ease the policy of permanent crisis he had inherited from Truman.

In January 1961, Eisenhower delivered his farewell address to the American people. His theme was the internal cost of the Cold War. His ideals were those of the small town in the Middle West where he grew up. He was afraid that big government and the regimentation of private life were threatening the old American values. He had no precise idea of what could be done about the dangers, for he knew that a huge defence establishment was necessary to carrying on the Cold War, but he did want to warn his countrymen. He pointed out that the 'conjunction of an immense military establishment and a large arms industry, . . . new in American experience,' exercised a 'total influence . . . felt in every city, every state house, every office of the federal government. . . . In the councils of the government, we must guard against the acquisition of unwarranted influence, whether sought or unsought, by the military-industrial complex.'

That his warning went unheeded by his successors goes without saying. They have also ignored another warning from this great champion of peace. On 31 August 1959, in an interview with Harold Macmillan on BBC TV, Eisenhower declared that peace was the total and immediate 'imperative'. And then he added, 'I believe that the people in the long run are going to do more to promote peace than any governments. Indeed, I think that people want peace so much that one of these days governments had better get out of their way and let them have it.'

FURTHER READING

The literature on Eisenhower is massive. Perhaps the best account of his childhood is Kenneth Davis, *Soldier of Democracy* (New York, 1952). Eisenhower's wartime career can be studied in his own *Crusade in Europe* (New York, 1948), or in Stephen Ambrose, *The Supreme Commander: The War Years of General Dwight D. Eisenhower* (New York, 1970). On the Presidency, see Eisenhower's memoirs, *The White House Years* (2 vols., New York, 1963), and Robert L. Branyan and Lawrence H. Larsen (eds.), *The Eisenhower Administration: A Documentary History* (New York, 1971). The best biography to appear to date is Peter Lyon, *Portrait of a Hero* (Boston, 1974).

Charles de Gaulle

JOHN C. CAIRNS

'Therefore the man who forces a way to power is commonly more fit for it in some respects than the man who finds a way. But this quality of man being rare, the case seldom occurs, unless under other circumstances of political commotion and subversion.'

Sir Henry Taylor

'I do not fear de Gaulle's arrogance. He knows he is going to die and that he will come to judgement.'

Pierre Emmanuel

'Fortune . . . singled me out to entrust me with the mighty venture which could have reshaped the face of the world: she changed me into a political man.'[1] These might have been, but were not, the words of Charles de Gaulle. They are in fact the words of a man he much admired, whose writing he emulated, and with whose literary skill his own was sometimes compared, Chateaubriand. De Gaulle, too, changed careers, apparently dramatically, and the sudden appearance of this soldier on the world stage far exceeded in its physical, moral and emotional impact the 'mighty venture' to which Chateaubriand thought Fortune had summoned him. Only specialists argue much now about Chateaubriand's political career. For de Gaulle it is different, but we may wonder whether such a time will ever come for him.

His reputation, living, was characterised by great swings of opinion, for and against. He was extravagantly praised and extravagantly denounced. Editorialists wore themselves out on him. Admiration vied with ridicule. Among the older generation, a President of the United States entertained his friends and colleagues with vulgar mimicry, summing up his incomprehension, suspicion, frustration, fury and distaste with a laconic, 'He's a nut.'[2] Roosevelt's Secretary of State hated

135

him implacably. The Prime Minister who first took de Gaulle up and supported him ('raised him from a pup', was the wartime phrase Churchill used[3]) had many times to be restrained from his more violent impulses to break with him, accusing him even of a capacity for treachery: 'He has been battening on us and is capable of turning round and fighting with the Axis against us.'[4] Twenty-five years later, other men with whose post-war dreams or ambitions de Gaulle came into collision were no less harsh, not least those who saw him as the 'gravedigger' of European unity. 'He is an accident,' Paul-Henri Spaak would say, 'perhaps a stupendous accident, but all the same transitory. Because of that he is not a truly great man, though he remains an exceptional personage.'[5]

Doubtless all of these men had some acquaintance with *Hamlet* and the definition there (Act 4, scene 4) of 'that capability and god-like reason' men are given to do great things. What they found hard to bear (without clearly perceiving it) was that this obscure soldier, a mere refugee from Hitler's Europe, should appropriate Hamlet's musings. And what they did not know (there is no evidence that any of them had ever read a word of de Gaulle's early writings, nor that they ever rectified this condition) was that he had long ago taken those thoughts to heart. He alluded to them all his days.

> . . . Rightly to be great
> Is not to stir without great argument,
> But greatly to find quarrel in a straw
> When honour's at the stake. . . .

As he saw it, the whole point of his life was in having found and having become the champion of 'une grande querelle'. Disabused about personal ambition in history, he disapproved of those who overstepped the limits. 'Napoleon', he wrote, 'exhausted the good will of Frenchmen, abused their sacrifice, covered Europe with graves, mortal remains, and tears. . . . Tragic revenge of the principle of restraint, legitimate wrath on the part of Reason.'[6] Thus he cast himself as mere instrument; this was his ultimate alibi. 'Throughout my life,' he said in the last months, 'what I have done was determined by circumstances. Of course I prepared myself for it and I had something to do with it. But in the end I have been above all an instrument.'[7]

Others, of course, saw it all otherwise, especially those who had once backed him but who had themselves long since been overtaken by events and by his achievements. 'De Gaulle,' Paul Reynaud remarked one day to the British Ambassador, 'is the victim of his talent for expression. He is drunk with the perfection of his presentation. He is a Saint-Cyrien who succeeded in politics.'[8] It was true, he was a Cyrard, he succeeded in politics. And there was a certain truth in what Pétain used to say: 'It was Paul Reynaud who turned his head.'[9] But what kind of soldier and politician he was is more difficult to tell.

The word 'military', Kurt Lang has written, implies 'an acceptance of organised violence as a legitimate means for realising social objectives.'[10] The spareness of such a definition suggests the limitations a man like de Gaulle might see in the profession of arms in our time. Everything we know about his youthful dreams and fantasies says that he sought something larger. It was after all significant that a sixteen-year-old boy, winning first prize in a local poetry contest for his somewhat melodramatic verses, should have rejected cash in favour of publication.[11] Nevertheless, it was the 'grandeurs et servitudes' of the Army that he chose. In those pre-1914 days, he remembered, the Army 'was one of the greatest things in the world. Beneath all the criticisms and insults which were lavished on it, it was looking forward with serenity and even a muffled hopefulness to the approaching days when everything would depend on it.'[12] This was certainly so in the last years of the nationalist preparation for war. What also was true was that, when it came, the war turned out to be an heroic but mindless butchery. There was no glory for Lieutenant de Gaulle. He was wounded in August 1914, again in February 1915, again in March 1916. Then followed five internment camps and thirty-two months as prisoner of war. There is some suggestion that already he thought of the political world.[13]

If there had been hard times for the Army before 1914, the post-1918 years were difficult in other ways. Unhappy police actions in Germany, budgetary restraints, a scaling down of the period of military service, a whole climate of opinion responsive to other values. 'These are hard days for authority,' de Gaulle noted as the thirties began.[14] Some officers were so discouraged as to write about *Feue l'Armée française*.[15] Many young men were less willing in the new era to accept what before 1914 had seemed to be 'la misère dorée'.[16] And many of them turned in their commissions. De Gaulle, however, stayed on. But he did not take the road to the colonies that attracted men such as his classmate Alphonse Juin; after Pascal Grousset, he repeated, 'Colonies are a school for pronunciamientos.'[17] He saw Syria and sensed that the end was coming. He never knew the spell that Morocco cast over his contemporaries, or even over younger men.[18] Like them, however, he was critical of his superiors and of what they had to teach. He himself was a success teaching military history at Saint Cyr, 'young, elegant in yellow boots, breeches and pastel blue tunic — [he] held forth in rolling periods on the policies of Richelieu, Mazarin and the Treaty of Westphalia,' André Beaufre recalled. 'I was profoundly struck by this course which cut across everything which I had learnt before.'[19] But he was evidently tiresome to those seeking to instruct him at the Ecole de Guerre in 1922-24. A now famous story tells how after a tactical field exercise he refused to give an explanation requested and referred the question to his 'chief of staff'. Being pressed, de Gaulle replied: 'Colonel, you entrusted me with responsibility for command of an army corps. If, in addition, to that, I had to assume the responsibilities of my subordinates, my mind would never be sufficiently free to carry out my mission. "De minimis non curat praetor. . . ." Chateauvieux, please answer the colonel's question. . . .'[20] He had marked down for such behaviour and it was then that his attachment to Pétain stood him in good stead. Unforgiving and contemptuous, he took literary revenge. ' "Arrogant and undisciplined",' he wrote in a piece of blatant autobiography only a few years later, 'is what the mediocrities say of [the man of character].'[21]

Such tales became part of de Gaulle's legend. But it would be wrong to see him as an entirely unorthodox soldier. He disliked the barracks for its lack of intellectual qualities. 'Alas, as you know,' he reported to his friend Lucien Nachin in late 1922, 'people in the Army now as in former days have no taste for serious thought. Routine, the love of insensate work, well named staff work, diverts their minds all too easily.'[22] Yet so far as serious thought was concerned, in the twenties de Gaulle himself suggested something close to military orthodoxy. 'Close off the highways,' he wrote to Nachin again in January 1927; 'that was what Vauban wanted done and I persist in thinking that what he achieved in the North mightily affected our enemies' mobility at the end of Louis XIV's reign and in 1792-93.'[23] As late as that date, then, when European military thought was already being renewed, he showed no great innovativeness. Perhaps it could hardly have been otherwise when his protector was still Marshal Pétain, although that particular *piston* was shortly to lose its force, if not to be entirely withdrawn. Still, it was under the aegis and in the presence of this prestigious man that de Gaulle gave his lectures in the Ecole de Guerre, April 1927,[24] which so irked the officers who had to sit through them. Whatever they announced, it was not new doctrine, though they achieved the *tour de force* of simultaneously paying all too blatant homage to the Marshal and celebrating those who broke with military dogma.

It was only years later when he had moved into a circle including an elderly lieutenant-colonel, Emile Mayer, whose influence on him appears to have been exceptional, that de Gaulle shifted from reflections on Vauban toward the conception of a French professional Army. Mayer encouraged him to publish a sketch of it in the spring of 1933. The book, *L'Armée de métier*, followed in 1934. What it contains of doctrine is derivative and imprecise. It is obviously addressed far more to politicians and an instructed general public than to soldiers. Almost as much as the Ecole de Guerre lectures, incorporated in *Le Fil de l'épée* (1932), it belongs in the province of moral at least as clearly as in the field of military thought. Both books mark the emergence of this professional soldier from the military classroom into the public arena where the state of the nation, the prospects of France in Europe and the world were being debated. Neither work had more than minimal sales. They were, however, widely reviewed, and Lieutenant-Colonel de Gaulle continued methodically to establish contacts with the press and with politics. The compulsion to reach a wider audience was pronounced. 'Indeed,' he would write shortly before his death, 'in all the sayings and writings that have accompanied my actions, what else have I myself ever been but someone endeavouring to teach?'[25]

As a career officer, he continued his normal duties. But he was both reshaping his thought and shifting his dependencies.

He achieved an oddly muted break with Pétain over literary matters, rejecting what he considered the inept meddling of his *patron* in the manuscript 'Le Soldat français de l'Ancien Régime à la Grande Guerre.' This was a work de Gaulle was putting together, from 1925 to 1927, for the Marshal's signature as credentials for election to the Académie Française. Pétain's emendation of a passage illustrated the abyss of principle and value separating the two men. De Gaulle wrote of the Revolutionary politicians stripping generals of 'prestige, often of life, sometimes of honour.' The Marshal transposed 'life' and 'honour.' De Gaulle reproved him: 'It's an ascension: prestige, life, honour.' Having taken his departure as *nègre*, he objected to other pens being employed on the manuscript. Pétain renounced his intention, and finally, in 1938, in defiance of the Marshal's wishes and editorial demands, de Gaulle published the revised work under his own name as *La France et son Armée*.[26] Neither this long drawn-out quarrel nor his eager and assiduous support of Paul Reynaud's parliamentary advocacy of an armoured force seems to have affected his career. His public pronouncements, however, and his known behind-the-scenes political activity, made him unacceptable to the Minister of War, Edouard Daladier, defender of the General Staff's views from 1936 to the catastrophe in 1940. Moreover, his scarcely veiled vituperation of some at least of his comrades in arms ('the stuffed dummies of the hierarchy,' 'weak-kneed creatures forever trembling in their shoes, jumping jacks who will turn their coats without scruple at the first opportunity'[27]) can have won him few friends.

In late 1937 he left the War Ministry for the 507th tank regiment at Metz. Thereafter, the outbreak of war in September 1939 took him to command the armour of the Fifth Army in Alsace. But there again he felt compelled to seek a wider audience for his views, sending to some eighty civil and military notables a memorandum on 'The Advent of Mechanised Power', on 26 January 1940. Ostensibly a plea for armoured divisions, it was in fact less a call for swift action in this domain than a vast prophesy of an imminent 'complete upheaval in the situation of peoples and the structures of States' consequent upon the 'political, social and moral crisis' through which France and the world were passing.[28] Though it appears to have had no effect at all, this extraordinary declaration by a soldier on active service was a mark of the exceptional times in which, as de Gaulle rightly judged, almost anything would be accepted, tolerated, from the exceptional man.

The story of de Gaulle's being summoned *in extremis* to take command of a sketchy 4th Armoured Division during the 1940 campaign is well known. Within weeks Paul Reynaud, Premier as of that March and in succession to Daladier, plucked de Gaulle from the battlefield to be Under-Secretary of State for National Defence. This was among the most important events of his life. Though their relations were to be broken very soon thereafter, as they took divergent paths in the wake of the debacle, and though a final violent breach occurred many years later when President de Gaulle outraged Reynaud (and almost every legal authority in France) by his changing the Constitution through referendum in 1965, still he would recall on Reynaud's death (September 1966), 'He was destiny's instrument for me. Belonging to his government, I became a political man. I left the military hierarchy. Having left the Army for public life that day, I never went back.'[29] He took to his new role with extraordinary ease. Within days, as the armies collapsed and the Government staggered toward its final crisis, de Gaulle was lecturing the Commander-in-Chief, General Maxime Weygand, on the civil-military relationship. Intellectually, he had been prepared for years. His first book, *La Discorde chez l'ennemi* (1924), had been a study of the nemesis that overtook Germany when Ludendorff violated the civil authority, destroyed the essential relationship subordinating the military régime, and so provoked 'the vengeance of principles flagrantly abused'.[30] Believing now that he saw Weygand and his generals about to do much the same thing, this temporary brigadier did not hestitate to reprimand the powerful old man for stepping out of his purely military role. As de Gaulle told it, he rejected Weygand's pessimistic views (10 June 1940), and to the Commander-in-Chief's retort, 'Have you something to suggest?', replied, 'The Government does not have suggestions to make, but orders to give.'[31] Only days earlier he had been a mere subordinate far down the line. Now he spoke for the civil power. From then on it was war to the knife between them. They never relented. And when Weygand died many years later in January 1965, at the age of ninety-seven, the younger man, President of the Republic, stepped in to prevent the funeral service being held in the church of Saint Louis des Invalides.[32] Long before the Armistice of 1940, de Gaulle had measured out the ground, perhaps written scenarios, certainly begun to put a certain distance between himself and the Army. Unlike Hindenburg, Franco and Eisenhower, he never held a supreme command; even as field commander his record remains in dispute.[33] Léon Noël remarked that he was always attached emotionally to the Army.[34] It might be more accurate to say that he was emotionally attached to the *idea* of the Army, the historic *role* of the Army, the *symbols* of the Army. For instance, if he was always scathing about Weygand, impugning his courage, subscribing to the legend of his being the child of the Emperor Maximilian's liaison with a Mexican dancer, hence suffering the incurable malady of having no French blood,[35] he was far more balanced about Pétain, the symbol of French victory in 1918. In private, de Gaulle often repeated that the Marshal had once been a great personage. Was he merely defending his own professional origins, conduct and judgement? Whatever the drama between them, de Gaulle's public pronouncements on Pétain after 1946 were delicate exercises in nuance and balance. Perhaps he had hoped that the old man would not return from Switzerland in 1944; he told the President of the High Court that he wanted a mild sentence of five years exile only; he always said that had he remained head of government, he would have sprung Pétain in a few years. But he was clear that the Marshal had to be condemned: he symbolised capitulation.[36]

Thus when the fiftieth anniversary of Verdun came round the nation held its breath. What would the President of the Republic say? The speech was full of nuance and almost impeccable: 'If, unhappily, in other times, in the late winter of his life and amid extreme events, the debility of old age brought Marshal Pétain to weaknesses that are to be condemned, the glory he had won at Verdun twenty-five years earlier . . . could be neither disputed nor disregarded by the country.'[37] But there was no relenting: Pétain's bones would not yet go to Douaumont. Privately, de Gaulle was harsh and would say, 'I saw Pétain die. . . . It was in 1925.'[38] Even in the last months of his own life, he maintained that he would have freed the old man: 'I would have sent the Marshal home, I would have pardoned him. What I condemn is what he represented: he was the symbol of a people that ceases to defend itself.'[39] In him the old Army had both triumphed and finally failed.

Of his own generation, de Gaulle appears to have felt affection for a few, not least for Marshal Juin, bitter though the break between them was on the Algerian affair. Juin, of course, was not a man of 18 June; he was converted from Vichy by the weight of the Allied invasion of French North Africa in 1942, which he initially opposed. But subsequently he kept the flag flying in the Italian campaign. The messages between him and de Gaulle were comradely: they had been together at Saint Cyr, they *tutoyéd* one another, and when, many years later, Juin lay close to death in Val de Grâce, the whole awful wreckage of Algeria between them, de Gaulle went to his bedside to encourage his friend.[40] Of younger men, some, like Raoul Salan, went into total opposition in the Secret Army Organisation. De Gaulle wanted his head, and when the High Military Tribunal would not deliver it in 1962, he dissolved that court and set up a new Military Court of Justice headed by his wartime companion General Edgard de Larminat. This frightful burden caused. Larminat to take his life: 'General,' he wrote the President, 'I am unable physically and mentally to carry out the duty set out for me. I am punishing myself, but I want it known that it is my weakness and not your strength and your clear-sightedness that are the cause.'[41] All the same, the unintentional indictment was obvious. Still it was significant that de Gaulle compelled obedience if not affection. General Jacques Massu, the celebrated 'victor' of the Battle of Algiers, publicly reprimanded for daring to criticise the President's policy and removed from his command, remained loyal. It was to Massu that de Gaulle flew in the final chaotic days of May 1968. Apparently it was Massu's assurances at Baden-Baden which led de Gaulle to decide to fight, to dissolve Parliament, hold elections and ride the backlash to victory over the opposition one last time.[42]

Clearly de Gaulle's relationship with the Army was complex. He loved the Army and he despised it. 'Mars,' he had written Nachin in 1927, 'was strong, handsome and courageous, but he was rather short of brains.'[43] Even so, old attitudes and responses were not so easily forgotten. Just before the generals' revolt in Algiers in April 1961, he would say that 'except for the Church, the Army was the only stable thing in France.'[44] This did not prevent his getting off blanket denunciations of the profession during the trying years before the Evian settlement. 'The French Army is always wrong,' he informed Jean Daniel in 1961; 'it was against Dreyfus, then for Pétain, and now it is for Algérie Française.'[45] Naturally he did not recall his own encouragements to this notion in the immediate aftermath of May 1958, the letter he had written to 'Mon cher Salan', 24 October 1958, for instance: 'The whole French nation is now united on a few simple ideas. We must not abandon French Algeria.'[46] Possibly André Malraux's observation is the right one, that de Gaulle was 'only incidentally a military man', that 'the military spirit influenced [him] in a profound but limited way.'[47] Equally, of course, his military reputation was at best in dispute before the events of 1940. The very cool reception he inspired among military men in the United Kingdom translated more than the prevailing distrust of French arms in the aftermath of defeat. 'I am told by everybody,' General Ironside noted, 'that he is an adventurer without any reputation in the Army.'[48]

He continued to speak of himself as a military man well into the war. Did he really believe this? One is tempted to think not. 'General I no longer am,' he remarked to Jules Moch one day in the spring of 1943. '. . . I am above the Army hierarchy.'[49] Rather it was essential for him to stress his limited soldier's role up to the point where he was assured of such solid support in occupied France that he could confront the hostile Roosevelt administration in his openly political guise. This was a long and bruising process. In a remarkable letter to Roosevelt, 26 October 1942, he begged for understanding and argued that if he now had some larger role, it had been thrust upon him by 'a sort of cult growing up in France, of which we were the centre'. He went on to say, 'I was not a politician. All my life I have remained loyal to my own speciality. When, before the war, I tried to interest the politicians in my ideas, it was on military grounds and for the sake of the country.' He had made his appeal 'as a soldier', but he could not now betray the people's hopes.[50] Whether Roosevelt and his advisers understood it or not (and everything indicates that they did not), de Gaulle was plainly putting forward the claim that the Army had made so many times and which he himself had set forth bluntly in *Vers l'Armée de métier* in 1934: 'the military corps is the most complete expression of a society.'[51] At the same time, his letter to Roosevelt was more cunning than convincing.

There is, nevertheless, evidence that de Gaulle sometimes still thought of himself as a soldier, a strategist, more particularly when the tide was turning in 1942. Twice that spring and summer he gave Ambassador Winant his views on the subject, while clearly giving notice that he had no intention of being drafted by anyone as a mere field commander. 'I am a French General. If the Allies ask me to play a military role I would not refuse. But it is not a simple matter.' Moreover, he said, the fact that they did not consult him 'shows that the Allies have no real wish to use what you call my military capacity.' His conception for an invasion of France involved landing on an extended front, testing the German defences to keep the enemy guessing, and then sending in the main force at some sector.[52] (As the Germans thought something like this was the scenario in 1944, it may be as well that de Gaulle's ideas were not seriously canvassed.) Washington made no effort to probe further, as de Gaulle's representatives there discovered. Across one document embodying his thought a State Department official wrote, 'It's not for a French General to express his opinion on this problem.'[53] And it is hard to think that this much troubled de Gaulle, though Gaston Palewski reported that de Gaulle's nervous state (in 1942) was owing to the fact 'that his military genius is left unused, that he is "pregnant with victory" and that he chafes at the idea that he could win the war in a few months and is not taken into our confidence.'[54] Extravagant as this may have sounded, Palewski may in fact have been merely repeating his leader's words, for shortly before his death the President told a visitor: 'But I knew what I was doing. It wasn't improvised. I had a policy for stopping Hitler. I had one for carrying the war victoriously against him. I had another for continuing it in June 1940. . . .'[55]

An old man's tales, or a frustrated resistance leader's fantasy — it makes no difference. No one enquired seriously for his strategic thought, and perhaps there was no reason why anyone should have: he was not a great captain. His opponents in Washington and London asked only that he get lost in the struggle with Hitler. 'Why doesn't de Gaulle go to war?' Roosevelt cabled Churchill jeeringly. 'Why doesn't he start

North by West half West from Brazenville? It would take him a long time to get to the Oasis of Somewhere.'[56] He had no intention of accommodating his enemies. For all practical purposes he had left the Army behind when Reynaud summoned him to Paris, when he flew off with Louis Spears to begin the struggle for recognition and for France. There was truth in Colonel Trinquier's bitter observation that 'except for a small Free French group which he promoted in a manner never known since the armies of the Revolution, the Army did not like him. The young officers did not know him; for them, de Gaulle was already an old symbol of the historic past.'[57] In some obscure manner, force of circumstances had opened the way to him and his preparations were uncannily advanced. He was more than Walter Mitty. 'You know,' he told his aide Claude Guy in May 1946, 'there was never a time in my life when I was not completely convinced that one day I should become leader of France. Only things did not turn out as I had expected. I always believed I should first be War Minister and that everything would start from there. . . .'[58] There is no reason to doubt this statement. His earlier writings had numerous references to the need for a new Louvois: 'Who will give the Republic a Louvois?' he asked his friends.[59] Perhaps, momentarily, he believed that Paul Reynaud might, but there can be no doubt that the famous portrait of the leader, the 'man of character', in *Le Fil de l'épée* bears an uncanny resemblance to the personage the General eventually launched upon the world. History, as uncertain a craft as one can find, ought not to rule out that great men may in some manner prepare their own reception if not their arrival. 'Nothing,' he once told a visitor, 'can be done without great men. And you become one only by wanting to be one.'[60]

What characterised the central condition in de Gaulle's prevision of his own destiny was catastrophe. Even with the materials now to hand, this catastrophic vision may be traced back to the nineteen-twenties. At the end of 1928 he confided to Lucien Nachin that the whole peace settlement would come tumbling down; that Poland would be attacked; that Germany would demand the return of Alsace-Lorraine. 'It seems to me to be written in the stars.'[61] This vision is characteristic of both *Le Fil de l'épée* and *Vers l'Armée de métier,* each with its plea for a great leader, a new Louvois, to guide the nation through the coming storm, for, as he put it in the closing line of the second book, 'The sword is the axis of the world and greatness cannot be shared.'[62] This dark reading of events is not less apparent in *La France et son Armée,* with its hypnotic concluding paragraph, the rhythms and tragic view of which would be elaborated, repeated and slightly altered on the final haunting page of his *Mémoires de guerre.*[63]

Jean Monnet once commented that de Gaulle 'has an odd technique. He always creates problems in order to solve them.'[64] This phenomenon, if it was such, was never more evident than in the bitter years after his resignation in January 1946. He had miscalculated; the Republic was established; there was no popular recall to power. His days appear to have been filled with a non-stop litany of the disasters, misfortunes, idiocies and incapacities on a global scale which could only portend parlaysis if not destruction for France. No doubt this was natural enough: princes, as Bacon noted, when checked in their desires, 'become secretly discontent, and look upon men and matters with an evil eye, and are best pleased when things go backward. . . .'[65] De Gaulle so little understood himself that he affirmed his taste for catastrophe while denying it. 'I'm perfectly content with my position,' he told one of his secretaries, Claude Mauriac, in the autumn of 1946; 'perfectly certain that I can't fail. But I don't like it! I'm not looking for political disasters. I should much prefer, for the country's sake, that I was mistaken about the future. If all goes well, it won't be I who obstructs them. I shall keep silent. . . . But I'm sure they won't succeed. I'm perfectly sure I shall win. . . .'[66] The nature and shape of the catastrophe predicted shifted in the years before 1958: now it was the spectre of Soviet armies rolling across Central Europe toward the Atlantic; now the internal collapse of the State from politics and subversion; now the oncoming *coup d'état* by an alienated Army erupting out of the ruins of an empire lost by quarrelling political pygmies. But always he described the same general progression: crisis, collapse of the regime, the appeal of de Gaulle. It would be nineteen-forty in a new guise. Nineteen-forty was the cardinal date in his life. He hever stopped talking about it. It was the grand, total crisis, the time when he had broken irreparably with the past, when he gathered new men around him, when he had set out on the major phase of his career.

'I found myself between two ages,' Chateaubriand wrote, 'as at the flowing together of two rivers; I flung myself into their roiling waters, moved regretfully away from the old bank where I had been born, swimming hopefully toward an unknown shore.'[67] This is one of the quintessential images of romanticism: you find it in Tocqueville,[68] and you find it in de Gaulle. De Gaulle certainly knew this passage in the *Mémoires d'outre-tombe*. And in *Le Fil de l'épée* there is an early expression of what was his master metaphor for the civil-military relationship. There he speaks with regret of the two solitudes: the busy life of the public man bowed beneath his own problems, and 'the life of the soldier, with its discipline and aloofness' which 'scarcely ever brings him into close contact with civil affairs. All the same' — de Gaulle continues — 'a vague sort of attraction does exist between the rulers and the generals. Seeing one another, on opposite towpaths of the same river, endlessly harnessed to the ship of their ambitions, these impassioned champions of authority are conscious of that deep, though unexpressed mutual respect which the strong feel for the strong. For all that, they remain on their own side of the stream. Their wishes, their anxieties, their activities are so different in kind, that they seldom, if ever, make contact.' He went on to say that 'an enlightened State' would do something to bring them together,[69] but this oblique appeal in the nineteen-thirties evoked no response. No government made such a move. Thus soldier and statesman were condemned to go on, each on his side of the river, eyeing one another, perhaps, with more suspicion than mutual respect.

So the years between the wars had run out; the crisis came; and like Chateaubriand, de Gaulle flung himself away from all he had known. 'I seemed to myself,' he wrote of his first day of the great adventure in London, 'alone as I was and deprived of everything, like a man on the shore of an ocean, proposing to swim across.'[70] Within days he had cast off for that distant shore which was both another world and another life. No doubt there were hesitations. Conditions were less than ideal. Hostilities abounded. Who will ever know the precise second thoughts and changing calculations de Gaulle endured in the first weeks? But despite the occasional reflections on a further military role already referred to, he never went back. A few years later, in Algiers, André Gide asked de Gaulle how he could have brought himself to disobey and set out on that transoceanic journey, but, as Malraux commented, the question was nonsensical to anyone who knew de Gaulle well.[71] That too had come to seem written in the stars.

As would-be statesman, what talents did he bring with him to the far shore? What ideas? The writings to that point reveal little of substance: it could all be summed up in a few phrases, an amalgam of old integral nationalism and a lofty awareness of the far regions of the globe; an attitude; a style. In retrospect, he seems to have been part of that general non-conformist groundswell of the thirties, protesting against the Republic as it was, stalemated, economically sclerotic, introversive, discouraged, resigned.[72] De Gaulle was against the system, against the class war, against the politics of disunity. He was above all a moralist, preaching renewal — first to the cadets at Saint Cyr, then to the officer corps at the Ecole de Guerre, finally to the nation. In London Roger Cambon, who had resigned from the diplomatic service rather than serve Vichy, but who was absolutely opposed to the General's venture, said flatly, 'Ideas? Why he has none.' Political doctrine? 'But he has none. His ambition — we know what his ambition is. But his ideas? None!'[73] In the beginning there was a good deal of truth in this, but as the war progressed de Gaulle spoke of 'revolution'. This was in part an echo from the thirties, and in part a necessary, if rather *pro forma*, response to the by the generic demand that the sacrifice of war be justified by large-scale post-war reform. It was also a reflection of the view held in London, as on the Continent, that Europeans must be raised against Hitler if the German empire was to be destroyed. 'Betrayed by her ruling and privileged classes,' de Gaulle said in early 1942, France had 'embarked on the greatest revolution in all her history.' She would be guided by 'new men', not the 'outworn politicians, sleepy academicians, intrigue-hardened businessmen and promotion-wearied generals' who had led her to defeat.[74]

It was all no more than a generalised vision of spiritual renewal, but it could not remain so. Force of circumstances defined reality and compelled de Gaulle to make choices, take action, give hostages to fortune. To broaden his support in metropolitan France and press his case for recognition by the Allies, he had eventually in London and Algiers to welcome back many outworn politicians, sleepy academicians and intrigue-hardened businessmen, even promotion-wearied generals. Moreover, his own immediate entourage was so divided socially and politically that a programme could not have been very clearly defined. After June 1944, in liberated France and responsive to the Resistance Charter, he agreed to various nationalisations but drew back from thorough-going economic and financial reconstruction. Pierre Mendès-France, his Minister of National Economy, condemned his course of action as choosing the easy way out, 'a policy which inevitably favours those who were enriched by the war, the speculators and profiteers, whilst it strikes at a number of poorer people. . . .'[75] The fact was that de Gaulle was not then and never had been ready for 'revolution'. What concerned him was the restoration of authority of the State; what he wanted was subordination of the parties to a strong executive branch. Cambon's judgement was less than fair. De Gaulle both knew what he wished to bring about and had an idea: France restored as a great power, her empire intact about her, her politics disciplined as they had not been, her ruling elite renewed: 'la Republique pure et dure'. Less than a precise blueprint, it was more than personal ambition.

Like all moral visions, it was a tall order. In the nearly thirty years he was on the world stage, half of them in office, he saw some of his hopes realised and some carried away by 'the gale of the century'. The greatest triumph he had was the triumph of Free France, the imposition of himself and his companions on the Allies, backed by a Resistance movement he had come to master; the determined rejection of British and American plans to introduce Allied Military Government of Occupied Territories into liberated France; the revival of the Republic in the name of his own entirely self-conferred 'legitimacy' stemming from 1940; the presence of France among the victors of the Second World War. 'Our Free France', he wrote a companion shortly before his death, 'was something great. We have never done anything better than that . . .'[76] Of all its campaigns, the greatest, most decisive was that against the foes in Washington and London, the battle against Roosevelt's inflexible position that he would preserve from Gaullist dictatorship the French people's right to self-determination, and Churchill's repeated demand that de Gaulle make accommodation with the American stand. Whatever he 'owed' them for sustaining him in their common interest, how could he accept the dictates of these meddling foreigners? how defer to allies who consistently kept open the line to Vichy and took grave decisions and actions, without consulting him, about the French Empire? Of Armand Annet, Governor General in Madagascar (which British forces seized), with whom Churchill wished to make peace, the Prime Minister was reported as saying, 'Annet's quite a good chap: Clemmie met him in a train somewhere once.'[77] Evidently foreigners with such an approach to the interests of France had to be resisted at all costs.

Next to the epic of Free France one might name de Gaulle's mastery after 1958 of the internal threat to the Republic brought on by the ruinous wars in the empire. It was not that he had by then abandoned his original vision of imperial France restored and so liquidated the empire. Almost anyone could have done that. It was that while finally coming to see that it must be done he simultaneously beat back the resulting civil and military rebellion which might have destroyed the democratic Republic. A third achievement was in persuading the French to accept and apparently to keep a form of government which broke with a long tradition, which was originally tailored to his measurements, but which ordinary mortals seem to be able to make work, and which, for all its failures — most dramatically revealed in 1968 — has provided a degree of ministerial stability that previous régimes did not. Finally, it could be said that if the rank and place which he sought for France in the post-war world were beyond her strength, still he helped restore her to a high level of prestige after 1958. And by so much he flung out a challenge to the super-powers in Europe and elsewhere which could conceivably encourage lesser nations one day to find a more sensible international order than that which the rival imperialisms of Russia and America proposed.[78] Such a design was almost endlessly bewildering to Americans: 'For God's sake,' Lyndon Johnson said one day to Maurice Schumann, 'tell me once and for all what General de Gaulle wants!'[79] They did not know, or did not understand the significance of the gesture de Gaulle made during the abortive summit conference of May 1960: after Khruschev had staged his scene, the French President touched Eisenhower's elbow and said, 'Whatever happens, *we are with you.*'[80]

None of de Gaulle's achievements, we may think, was carved

in stone. He had his outright failures, too. Formally at war with the Germans, he was primarily at odds with the Allies.[81] Although he sent de Lattre to sign the surrender documents in Berlin, he himself had to acknowledge defeat in the imperial domain at the hands of Great Britain: France's extrusion from Syria was doubtless certain, but he believed, with some justification, that his benefactor-enemy had taken advantage of France's misfortune to end once for all the imperial rivalry in the Levant. By 4 June 1945 tension was so great that he had warned General Beynet in Beirut that 'the English may really employ force against us. In this case we must reply with force, whatever may be the outcome.' It did not come to that, but at his press conference two days earlier, asked whether Britain was responsible for France's troubles there, he had said only, 'We will leave that for history to decide.'[82]

His worst failure was self-inflicted: the misadventure of the RPF movement after 1946, a strident, flashy, noisy demagogic attempt to discredit the Fourth Republic and ride the whirlwind of supposed Communist subversion and an imminent Russian invasion of Central and Western Europe. In his frustration at not being recalled to power he even considered and rejected the possibility of *coup d'état*.[83] 'A *coup d'état*?' he would say in those years. 'But one can't carry out a *coup d'état* without having public opinion on one's side.' Or, 'I've too much respect for France to present her with some kind of South American pronunciamiento.'[84] If he had men around him who were less scrupulous, he never gave them their head. 'For me,' André Malraux would say, 'the RPF was in insurrectional movement. . . . but de Gaulle is not a man of violence. He's a man of great decisiveness, which isn't the same thing'[85] And by 1953 the RPF was in ruins, collapsed of its own inability to bring about the crisis of the Fourth Republic which would open the way to the extraordinary man. De Gaulle was reduced to waiting on catastrophe once more.

Of his failures as President of the Fifth Republic it is less easy to speak with assurance. If he seriously hoped to be admitted to an Atlantic partnership, that ambition was denied him. But he would argue that the September 1958 memorandum to Eisenhower and Macmillan was only a device: 'I was then looking for a way to get out of the Atlantic Alliance and to regain the freedom of action that had been surrendered by the Fourth Republic. . . . Hence I asked for the moon, I was sure they would not give it to me.'[86] But was his thought quite so clear? Nothing we know about him permits us to feel sure. If he hoped to bind the Federal German Republic to France and so create a Continental nucleus of power with which to confront Russia and America, he knew how fragile was the relationship achieved and that once the old Chancellor had gone the extraordinary bond they had created between them would cease. As Harold Macmillan noted, 'Poor Adenauer . . . usually "sucks up" to de Gaulle.' His successors were different. 'He'd have his feet dyed green,' de Gaulle remarked in disgust of Ludwig Erhard, 'if Washington asked him.'[87] And if he hoped, as he was during the war, to force the United States to recognise him and what he was — what *France* was — by making time with the Soviet Union, all he got in Russia was ceremony, protocol, technical accords and agreeable words. Brezhnev and his colleagues were no less realistic than Stalin had been: they knew it and he knew it: France had only fifty million people. Despite his extraordinary personal representation of the mission of France from Warsaw to Mexico City to Phnom Penh, there were fundamental limitations which denied even the exceptional man prizes reserved — if for anyone — for the super-powers.

On the domestic scene, beyond the *domaine réservé* of foreign affairs (which, his protests to the contrary,[88] was the area which truly interested him, however hard he worked at other matters), his achievements and failures may well have balanced out. He inherited in 1958 a basically sound economy, he brought about an essential currency reform, he backed a successful programme of rural modernisation. But when he sought to go beyond capitalism — and this was an ambition with its roots going back to those non-conformist stirrings in the nineteen-thirties —• he made no obvious progress: the notion of participation, a vague formula suggesting some way round the endless employer-employee struggle, was opposed by almost all his advisers. He saw it as 'a means to reawaken the country, to make it aware of itself, in a word, to shake it up!' He saw it as a symbol of the change that must come in the industrial sphere. 'Participation', he told Malraux, 'was the road we would take, feeling our way, to this transformation. And you know that in voting against me France didn't brush aside the Regions, the Senate and all that: she dismissed what participation symbolised. I said what I had to say. But the game was over.'[89]

Failures acknowledged, the performance was all the same extraordinary. How had he brought it off? Machiavelli held 'that fortune is the author of one half of our action, but that she still leaves us to direct the other half, or perhaps a little less.'[90] De Gaulle put it a little differently. Sometimes he said that 'History is moved by forces which, for the most part, are beyond the control of politicians, however great they may be.' Toward the end he would say, 'ultimately I was above all an instrument.'[91] Like Machiavelli, he accepted the fact that great men were helpless without the support of the people. But de Gaulle's conception of the relationship was more complex: he knew that in the twentieth century, at least, a prince, risen 'through the favour of the people', could not keep them in a friendly disposition merely by not oppressing them.[92] Unlike Machiavelli, he made a distinction between an idealised and historic 'people' (almost an abstraction in the romantic view of Michelet) and the people who were his contemporaries. Somehow these two blended, and yet they were distinct. With the 'people' as the historic reality of France and of which the State was the permanent manifestation he had, as everyone knows, a lifelong love affair. With his contemporary Frenchmen there was no love affair. 'France is above the French,' he would say. 'I did not busy myself about the happiness of the French. One dies for France: that shows that she is something else and something more than the French.'[93]

Between him and contemporary Frenchmen, however, there was a contract. Or rather, the contract was mysteriously sealed between him and France, with the French having the power to break it. In de Gaulle's view, they broke it twice.[94] Naturally, he was blameless. If he was aloof and unresponsive to them, it was not because (as Machiavelli might have said) it was better to be feared than loved. 'A leader', the General explained, 'can only be faithful to the nation and not to any particular citizens or class of citizens. As for love, it is a two-way street, or it becomes a dead-end alley, cluttered with the ugly debris of un-requited emotion. A leader cannot give love, therefore he must not accept it, for love unrequited turns to hate.'[95] It was one of special qualities of Charles de Gaulle to be able to speak in this way without any self-consciousness, as if the democratic revolution of the modern world had not swept such rhetoric from the public stage, as if the Fascist mumbo-jumbo of the first half of the twentieth century had not ended in global tragedy. France, he insisted, understood all this that he felt and gave voice to; his contemporaries did not. His scorn for them was withering and his prognosis of their condition bleak. After all, he had experienced what Machiavelli had only written about: 'The worst that a prince may expect from a hostile people is to be abandoned by them.'[96] Following the unsuccessful referendum of April 1969, he was capable of withdrawing momentarily into something like self-pity: 'I was wounded in May 1968. And now they've finished me off.'[97]

As 'l'instrument désigné' under contract to France, who was de Gaulle and how did he function? Crudely put, he was a rebellious colonel (temporarily raised to the rank of brigadier-general) launched on the world by Winston Churchill's friend Louis Spears, with the assistance of Desmond Morton, one of Churchill's secretaries, and the services of Richmond Temple, and advertising man retained by Major Morton, on of Churchill's secretaries, and the services of Richmond Temple, an advertising man retained by Major and interviews.[98] There was a good deal of early resistance to him. Few but the Prime Minister and the group round him were enthusiastic. Neville Chamberlain noted that de Gaulle 'seems a stout fellow' who 'may succeed in forming a new government here as a rallying point',[99] but the Foreign Office and the War Cabinet thought better of that.[100] They hoped for the arrival of better-known *émigrés* who might rally the empire away from the Marshal and back into the war. Before long a certain note of disparagement sounded: 'Still no Frenchmen blowing any trumpets anywhere except de G. in London,' Hugh Dalton observed late in June 1940, 'and his trumpet blasts are becoming a bit monotonous.' By then the Chief of the Imperial General Staff informed the Prime Minister that he did not wish any Frenchmen in the United Kingdom and that he hoped that they would all go home. Churchill was furious,[101] but the backlash of disenchantment with France and the ridicule of the self-proclaimed standard-bearer were setting in. 'I can't tell you anything about de Gaulle.' Sir Alexander Cadogan told his Foreign Office colleagues after a first meeting with de Gaulle, 'except that he's got a head like a pineapple and hips like a woman.'[102] Thus, having launched him as a fighting soldier, they drew back from commitment to him as a political figure. They hoped almost endlessly to see General Weygand or Edouard Herriot or any major figure come out of France to assume leadership and subordinate de Gaulle to him. But no one came. And those who did arrive in London from the empire, like the senior General Georges Catroux, were too loyal to de Gaulle to accede to British blandishments.[103] The ultimate candidacy of General Henri Giraud, Roosevelt's last best hope, proved to be the occasion for tempestuous quarrels before it collapsed as a result of Giraud's political ineptitude and de Gaulle's political skill.

Beyond the mundane immediate circumstances of his appearance as leader of the Fighting French in London, however, de Gaulle's strength lay in the rapid assumption of a persona which for the rest of his life he considered independent of his private self. 'De Gaulle', he would say, 'interests me only as a historical personality.'[104] He was not always careful to distinguish between the first and third person when speaking of de Gaulle the instrument, though the initial effect on others, whichever form he used, was electrifying. Hence Harold Nicolson's astonishment at a Savoy luncheon in January 1941 when, vainly denying the Ministry of Information's supposed Pétainist sympathies and insisting, 'Nous travaillons pour la France entière,' he heard the General shout at him, 'La France entière, c'est la France libre. C'est moi!'[105] If it did not seem funny, it seemed bizarre. Some thought it outrageous: 'Walking along in St James's Street after lunch,' noted that egregious and amusing snob, Sir Henry Channon, 'I met de Gaulle . . . strutting along insolently, and . . . crossed over to avoid [him]. Nobody can stomach de Gaulle. His intolerable swagger and conceit infuriate everyone.'[106] Washington and London sniggered about Joan of Arc, the smell of smoke, and so forth. Rival French exiles pronounced him 'untruthful, treacherous and unbalanced'.[107]

Whatever his clinical condition, however, his behaviour showed great constancy. Evidently he meant seriously what he said, then and all his life long. And now one must ask, was it so hard to understand? 'What', he said to an Albert Hall audience in 1942, 'could have become of the country had Joan of Arc,

Danton, or Clemenceau been willing to come to terms?'[108] Was it so absurd to think of them at such a time? What was certainly more difficult to absorb was the separateness of the historic persona de Gaulle. The General once explained that he himself had not understood what had happened until he went to Douala in French Equatorial Africa in October 1940. This was after the crisis of the abortive expedition to Dakar the previous month, the seaborne nature of which had really been imposed on him by the British. He had acquiesced in the final arrangements and at the time he had silently accepted the principal blame. 'I went through a terrible time,' he told a friend. 'I even thought of blowing my brains out.'[109] Aboard the escort vessel *Commandant Duboc* taking him south from Lagos, he said quietly to the British liaison officer sitting beside him one evening, 'Pour moi ce qui est terrible, c'est de me sentir seul. Toujours seul.'[110] All the same, the arrival in Douala, where Major Leclerc greeted him, marked a turning point. There, on French soil, in Africa, crowds shouted his name, and a certain transformation seemed to have occurred in his mind. 'I realized then that General de Gaulle had become a living legend. . . . From that day on I knew I would have to reckon with this man. . . . I became almost his prisoner.'[111] Thereafter, in office or out, it made no difference, he insisted always on his legitimacy. It had been delegated to him in some mysterious process between June and October 1940, and so far as he was concerned, from then until the final breaking of the contract, it was as if the Etat Français of Vichy and the Fourth Republic had never been. As he remarked to Claude Mauriac in 1946, 'I'm always France.'[112]

All this might seem to lie in the province of higher lunacy, no doubt. Yet it worked; it was a reality. The tale of how it worked has been told many times, by him and by others. Not least astonishing was the enormous intransigence which sprang from almost total weakness and from an attitude of almost total suspiciousness of the British. Though free of the crude dislike manifested by the American leadership, Churchill repeatedly burst out against de Gaulle in violent terms: 'There is nothing hostile to England this man may not do once he gets off the chain.'[113] Hence the decision sometimes to keep him temporarily virtual prisoner in the United Kingdom. Half enraged, half admiring, during some of their worst difficulties when de Gaulle came close to being overthrown by his British supporters, Churchill remarked, 'His country has given up fighting, he himself is a refugee, and if we turn him down he's finished. Well, just look at him! Look at him! He might be Stalin, with two hundred divisions behind his words. . .. Perhaps the last survivor of a warrior race.'[114] The intransigence was felt by all. When de Gaulle's own representatives dared suggest that his threats to the Allies could only discredit the Free French cause, they received a stinging telegram of reprimand: 'In conclusion, I invite you to be firmer and not to give the impression that those who represent me do not follow my policy exactly. Our greatness and our strength consist solely in intransigence over what concerns the rights of France. We shall have need of this intransigence as far as the Rhine inclusive.'[115] He was as good as his word and his refusal to conform with the Allies' scenario before the Normandy invasion sent General Marshall into a towering (and finally absurd) rage with Anthony Eden, whose thankless task it was to try ceaselessly to mediate between de Gaulle, Churchill and the Americans.[116] That other American soldier, Marshall's subordinate, Eisenhower, learned to control his feelings about the General. Years later (when both were chiefs of state), Secretary of State Dulles, refusing to confront de Gaulle over what seemed to Washington to be a deliberate misrepresentation of United States diplomacy, quoted Eisenhower as saying, 'there's no point in getting into a pissing contest with a skunk.'[117] It is nevertheless true that it was this same intransigence which broke the Algiers rebellion in 1961, when he looked into the television camera to denounce this 'odious and stupid adventure' and to order 'in the name of France' that 'all means, I say all means, be used to bar the way everywhere to these men, until they are brought down.'[118]

Intransigence, craft, cunning, tools of the trade. 'Everyone admits how praiseworthy it is in a prince', wrote Machiavelli, 'to keep faith, and to live with integrity and not with craft. Nevertheless our experience has been that those princes who have done great things have held good faith of little account, and have known how to circumvent the intellect of men by craft, and in the end have overcome those who relied on their word.'[119] De Gaulle was lion and fox, 'a great pretender and dissembler'. Against some odds, he picked off his American-backed rival, Henri Giraud, in 1943-44, and despatched him into historical oblivion with a masterly, ironic encomium ('the government with sorrow respected his wish . . . a glory that will not fade'),[120] an exercise which conformed splendidly to the precept of that nineteenth-century observer of the way of men, Sir Henry Taylor, of whom most probably de Gaulle never heard: 'In the therapeutics of statesmanship the enmity of an assailant should be looked upon as a peccant humour, which is to be cured, first by a blister and then by a salve.'[121] No less deftly, de Gaulle lured the French Resistance into his camp and, once in liberated Paris, swallowed the movement whole, ridiculing it in the act: 'Remember,' Winston Churchill had minuted that spring, 'that there is not a scrap of generosity about this man. . .[122] In retrospect, it seems almost inconceivable that he could have taken in the politicians of the country in 1958 with flattery so wicked as to be almost worse than his genuine contempt for them. Of his balcony scenes, that of June 1958 at the Government General building in Algiers would appear within four years to have been consummately cynical. And yet the famous pronouncement, 'Je vous ai compris,' was more ambiguous than treacherous, if it was not simply statesmanlike. There is no reason to think he then foresaw what would happen at Evian in 1962.

His utterances were often so sibylline that they never ceased to be scanned for hidden meaning. Yet his thought was in many ways so fluid and opportunistic that it could not be readily seized. And now there is a kind of perverse fascination in the anxious diary entries of Harold Macmillan, wondering what this astonishing and almost inscrutable President of France was going to do. 'Sometimes when I am with him,' the Prime Minister wrote, 'I feel I have overcome it. But he goes back to his distrust and dislike, like a dog to his vomit.'[123] Then came the flat press conference declaration of January 1963, that 'England is, in effect, insular, maritime,' unfit for Europe.[124] At that time, the shock was great, though Machiavelli had warned that, 'He who believes that new benefits will cause great personages to forget old injuries is deceived.'[125]

De Gaulle's arsenal contained many weapons. Again and again, he held the French to ransom with his threat of abandoning them to the Communists, if not to the Russians — until finally the act wore out: evidently the Communists were a none too brilliant part of the political system, and no one much thought the Russians were coming. By the spring of 1968, the nation's response to him had slackened. But in the events of May and June, when the Communist Party roused itself lethargically to try to lead the revolt that had become something like anarchy, the French gave him a last mandate to restore order. Despite the Gaullist election success, the atmosphere had changed. His threats, like his manipulation of the word, held no more magic. Bored or not, the nation appeared largely indifferent to him.

The prince, Machiavelli had advised, 'ought to entertain the people with festivals and spectacles at convenient seasons of the year. . . .'[126] In a sense this had been done during the war as a matter of course. Thereafter, the mood of excitement had to be contrived. Malraux was pageant-master of the RPF, and his spectacles were half Hollywood, half Nuremberg. They scarcely survived the movement, however, and after the initial campaign for the new constitution in 1958 were not much seen. The General and his immediate entourage were less extravagantly inclined.[127] Nonetheless, de Gaulle had a keen appreciation of the impact his 'almost legendary person' made on the towns and cities he visited. From time to time, the travelling Presidential show erupted out of Paris to this region or that: the automobile cavalcade; the gaggle of local notables nervously awaiting the great man; the set speech about Lille or Toulon being the pride of France;[128] the Marseillaise; the 'bain des foules', plunging myopically into the crowd to grasp hands, even if only those of his security 'gorillas'; and then off to the next town at top speed. This sometimes bizarre and even ridiculous proceeding made no difference: de Gaulle had been there, they had actually seen him. And for a long time it worked.

The persona de Gaulle was so powerful that it could even commit with impunity what the legal bodies of the nation proclaimed to be flagrant violations of the constitution. In 1962, though challenged on every side, he carried his fight directly to the people in a referendum which solidly backed his constitutional revision to permit popular election of the President of the Republic. His determination then was matched only by his superb arrogance after in condemning the opposition 'in that I myself was the principal inspirer of the new institutions, and it really was the height of effrontery to challenge me on what they meant.'[129] He won that struggle hands down, but 1962 was the high point of his nearly eleven years as President. In 1958, propelled by conspiracy in Algiers (if not at Colombey-les-deux-Eglises, the story of which is not yet clear[130]), something like despair on the part of René Coty at the Elysée, and resignation finally in the Palais Bourbon, he had picked up power almost from the street. In 1965, François Mitterrand and the Left compelled him to fight for it. He was threatened in the National Assembly elections of 1967; he stumbled for weeks during the 1968 affair; and one may wonder whether fundamentally he chose to exit in 1969. The problem of existing preoccupied him endlessly. In the early days, during the war, such talk may have been dust scattered in men's eyes: 'As for me, I shall withdraw,' he remarked to a visitor in September 1944, '. . . I have a mission; and it is coming to an end. I must disappear. France may again one day have need of a pure image.'[131] But after 1965 his concern could only have been real. The 'late winter of life' loomed up, *le naufrage.*

'Princes', Bacon wrote, 'are like to heavenly bodies, which cause good or evil times; and which have much veneration, but no rest.'[132] In many ways, de Gaulle was a simple man, driven by a demon. From youth he had held the hope of accomplishing 'great enterprises and setting a fine example.'[133] Asked once what he considered his principal quality, he replied, 'modesty', and went on to explain: 'When you contain the destiny of France, you can never be great enough, strong enough or fine enough!'[134] No doubt this conception of self and mission accounted for his use of men, objectively, coldly, sometimes inhumanly. In reply to General Leclerc's evident combination of hesitation and gratitude on being appointed overall commander of Free French forces in Africa, March 1942, he telegraphed: 'Do not be intimidated by your rapid rise. My aim is not at all to give you pleasure, in spite of my friendship for you. . . . We are in a revolution. Only capacity justifies function and I am judge of that capacity.'[135] He did not hesitate to use Michel Debré to carry out the policy of Algerian disengagement, fully aware of the extreme burden this was on a man whose opposition to that policy was exceeded only by his loyalty to de Gaulle; and when Debré had been used up in the affair, he summarily replaced him as Prime Minister. Similarly, when Georges Pompidou had helped see the régime through the 1968 events, he was eliminated.

De Gaulle could be vindictive in petty ways; about grievances he discerned done to France he was implacable. Churchill remarked that England's offence was to have helped France: 'He cannot bear to think she needed help.'[136] There was truth in that view, but it was too narrow a reading: the essential quarrel was over the Allies' refusal to grant him full recognition from those early days when he had issued the Manifesto from Brazzaville on 27 October 1940 ('Events are imposing this sacred duty upon me. . . . I shall exercise my powers in the name of France. . . .'), together with the ringing ordinances, beginning, 'In the name of the French People and Empire, We, General de Gaulle, Leader of the Free French, Ordain. . . .'[137] That London and Washington would not take him at his own evaluation was the essential problem. Nearly twenty years later, Macmillan noted, 'He *hates* England — still more America — because of the war, because of France's shame, because of Churchill and Roosevelt, because of the nuclear weapon. Yet it is a "love-hate" complex.'[138] And that seemed nearer the mark. It showed in the memoirs and in his conversation, in his remarks as Churchill lay dying, in the rueful statement about his relationship with Eisenhower: 'Men can have friends. Statesmen cannot.'[139]

He could be merciless in the name of the State against those who touched France. One can rightly speak of a large-scale massacre of Algerian Moslems in the wake of some atrocities perpetrated on Europeans in Sétif on VE Day.[140] And his fury could be heightened by something like racism. 'These wogs', he remarked during the final convulsions in Algeria, 'aren't like us. Look at what they're doing. . . , mutilating and emasculating their victims. You can give them money and shower them with gold but they'll still piss on you in the end.'[141] To be fair, another side of his character was touched by the quality of mercy. He was said to have examined hundreds of dossiers in the post-1944 collaboration and treason trials.[142] And he was said to have felt a certain respect for the idealism of Colonel Bastien-Thiry, one of those who tried to assassinate him at Petit-Clamart, and who therefore had to die as the ritual of their 'duel' demanded. 'The French need martyrs,' de Gaulle said. 'They must choose them well. I could have given them one of those idiot generals, now playing football in the courtyard of Tulle prison. I gave him Bastien-Thiry. They can make a martyr of that one, if they want, when I've disappeared. He deserves it.'[143] Indeed, he had only contempt for soldiers like Salan and Jouhaud who, in his eyes, had betrayed the Army and the honour of France. Furious at Salan's escaping the death penalty, he was with difficulty prevented from insisting that General Jouhaud's death sentence be carried out.[144]

There were, of course, softer qualities in the private man. He liked children, he liked the movies, he liked Josephine Baker ('the poor good girl!'[145]), and he liked to eat, though the meals at the Elysée in his time were said to be terrible. Despite his reputation, he was willing on occasion to unbend and use the English language, against the invasions of which into his own tongue he never ceased to do battle. 'He spoke English remarkably well,' the Canadian Prime Minister observed in 1944.[146] He had and he knew how to exercise a talent for pleasing. 'Now that he is old and mellowed,' Macmillan remarked in 1960, 'his charm is great. He speaks beautiful, rather old-fashioned French. He seems quite impersonal and disinterested.'[147] But, as Macmillan would have occasion to see again, he could be much less forthcoming. In exile after the fall of France, he had so often been brittle to a degree, withdrawn, silent, stung by criticism and ridicule. Oliver Lyttelton thought the General must have risen each morning, saying to himself, 'France is dishonoured. Where and when am I going to be insulted today?' To his hostess in Cairo one day, who asked him what his interests were beyond war and politics, he replied barely smiling, 'Madame, je regarde le système solaire.'[148] He was not a humorous man, but he had a sharp wit. At a State dinner one evening in April 1962, Jacqueline Kennedy, whom he was said to have found engaging, turned to him to confide, 'You know, I come from an old French family.' 'Really,' was the reported response. 'So do I.'[149]

He was human, and while he may have been secretly delighted by the stories about him which made the rounds, he professed to think them unworthy. He disapproved of Lord Moran's published diary of the years with Churchill, portrait of the hero in bedroom slippers. What concerned him and what should seriously concern others was General de Gaulle, the historic de Gaulle, the soldier who crossed the river, swam the ocean to the far shore. That man was neither gracious nor charming. However much may have escaped him in the daily conduct of affairs, especially after 1958, he was master. The Council of Ministers meetings were severe. 'He fascinates the ministers,' Antoine Pinay remarked on leaving the Cabinet. 'No one dare speak.'[150] This was not quite true, but those who failed the test of compliance were summarily ousted or knew when to quit, as did Pierre Sudreau, protesting the constitutional revision procedure of 1962. To Sudreau's expressed fears that the use of the referendum might prove an unfortunate precedent, de Gaulle replied, 'Oh come now, Sudreau, no one will ever have the cheek to do what I'm doing.'[151] This de Gaulle, harsh, distant and aloof, skilfully hid the other, believing, as Georges Bidault once informed the United States Ambassador, that 'Frenchmen always try to please the man to whom they are talking. He thinks they overdo it and he adopts a different attitude. He makes no effort to please.'[152]

Perhaps he was one of those 'eminently meditative statesmen' whom Sir Henry Taylor thought the greatest he had known.[153] In many respects, though by no means in all, he met the requirements laid down by Taylor, Machiavelli and Bacon; and by the youthful de Gaulle. No doubt Fortune, his star, had a hand in it, but he was also his own work of art,[154] living the drama of the State in what he chose to regard as a Manichean world. He unquestionably had 'a certain taste for misfortune' (as Spaak said[155]), and an equivalent capacity for inviting fierce resentment and ridicule. Churchill once admonished Charles Peake, the long-suffering Foreign Office liaison officer to de Gaulle, 'I hold you responsible that the Monster of Hampstead does not escape.'[156] But the slings and arrows were no surprise to him. On his desk Zarathustra's uncompromising judgement stared at him: 'Alles ist leer, alles ist gleich, alles war.'[157] This man, with the narrowest concept of greatness, yet so free from the public meannesses of his time, posing always as the tireless servant of the State, fixedly believed himself to have been marked out by destiny to bear France on his shoulders, 'to guide her upwards, while all the voices continued to call her down.'[158] Yet he was also a nay-sayer. He had a taste not only for misfortune, but for catastrophe, too. 'Ah, the General is seventy-six,' his *chef de cabinet* once said to Harold Wilson, 'and has little to look forward to.'[159] Predicting that things would fall apart after him, that the age of giants was over, he would parade his disenchantment, hold forth time after time on taking his exit. 'What's the point of hanging on?' he remarked in the aircraft returning him from Eisenhower's funeral. 'One must know when to leave and isn't this the time to do it?'[160] But like every other actor, he postponed his final curtain.

He thought also of his death, and perhaps it was natural that he should have thought of the death of another soldier who had crossed the river to politics. One day he told his son Philippe that Hindenburg had said to his own son, 'When the Angel of Death arrives, you will tell me'; and that as the old man had laid abed dying he had asked, 'Is he in the house?'; and that the son had replied, 'No, in the garden, but he will soon come in.' De Gaulle said to Philippe, 'I shall put the same question to you.'[161] It did not turn out that way, of course. He was struck down suddenly, without warning, early one evening in the autumn of 1970. The end was very quick and very simple.[162]

The country had already, as before in 1946, learned to live without him. If in fact he deliberately sought the exit of which he talked so much, he chose to cast it as rejection. 'I can do nothing more,' he had told Debré even before the referendum took place. 'The people want nothing more of me. There's nothing for me to do but leave.' And having recorded his last television address the next day, he said, 'All that is perfectly useless. C'est foutu.'[163] In the concluding year and a half of his life he had found all that hard to bear. So he alternated between a distant hopefulness that one day other men would move on to 'climb the heights', inspired by his example, and an insistent expression of failure: 'I'm the character in Hemingway's *Old Man and the Sea:* I've brought back only a skeleton.'[164]

Maybe more than most soldiers and statesmen he knew that there are no final victories and that the verdict on him would have to wait on history. It was nevertheless hard for him to come to terms with that. Hence the endless monologues, the questioning of all who came to Colombey, 'What are they saying in Paris?'[165] He must have known that in Paris they had virtually ceased to speak of de Gaulle. General de Gaulle, the extraordinary combination of military and civil qualities he embodied, belonged to the past. He knew it, had said so himself, but how could he accept it? And about all that the words of Henry Adams years before are as good as any: 'The inevitable isolation and disillusionment of a really strong mind — one that combines force with elevation — is to me the romance and tragedy of statesmanship.'[166]

NOTES

1. Chateaubriand, *Mémoires d'outre-tombe*, 2 vols (Paris, Flammarion, 1950), I, pp.249-50.
2. 1 July 1944. William D. Hassett, *Off the Record with FDR 1942-1945* (New Brunswick, New Jersey, 1958), p.257.
3. 'Churchill spoke very contemptuously of the vanity, pettiness and discourtesy of de Gaulle, saying he had raised from a pup but that he still barked and bit,' 22 May 1943. *The Price of Vision: The Diary of Henry A. Wallace 1942-1946*, John Morton Blum (ed.) (Boston, 1973), p.202.
4. 21 November 1942, *The Diaries of Sir Alexander Cadogan 1938-1945*, David Dilks (ed.) (New York, 1972), p.496; cf. Cadogan's entry for 5 June 1944: 'Roosevelt, P.M. and — it must be admitted de G. — all behave like girls approaching the age of puberty. Nothing to be done.' Ibid., pp.634-5. This was when the worst scenes between de Gaulle and Churchill seem to have occurred, though accounts are far from full. See André Gillois, *Histoire secrète des Français à Londres de 1940 à 1944* (Paris, 1973), pp.7-31; Earl of Avon, *The Eden Memoirs*, 3 vols. (London, 1960-65), II, pp.452-7, a very guarded account; Sir Llewellyn Woodward, *British Foreign Policy in the Second World War*, 3 vols. (London, 1970-71), III, pp.51-61; Winston S. Churchill, *The Second World War*, 6 vols. (Boston, 1949-53), V, pp.628-30; Charles de Gaulle, *War Memoirs*, 3 vols. (London, 1955-61), II, pp.226-31.
5. Paul-Henri Spaak, *Combats inachevés*, 2 vols. (Paris, 1969), II, pp.164, 166.
6. Charles de Gaulle, *La France et son Armée* (Paris, 1938), p.150.
7. To Jean-Marcel Jeanneney, quoted in Jean Mauriac, *Mort du Général de Gaulle* (Paris, 1972), p.125.
8. November 1964, quoted in Piers Dixon, *Double Diploma: The Life of Sir Pierson Dixon, Don and Diplomat* (London, 1968), p.311.
9. Guy Raissac, *Un Combat sans merci: l'affaire Pétain-de Gaulle* (Paris, 1966), p.238.
10. Kurt Lang, 'Military', *International Encyclopedia of the Social Sciences* (New York, 1968), X, p.305, col. 1.
11. J.-R. Tournoux, *Pétain et de Gaulle* (Paris, 1964), 28 fn; Jean Lacouture, *De Gaulle* (New York, 1968), p.16.
12. Charles de Gaulle, *War Memoirs*, I, p.10.
13. Lacouture, *De Gaulle*, p.28; see Jean Pouget, *Un certain Capitaine de Gaulle* (Paris, 1973), pp.67-128. Note, however, his remark to Robert Murphy at Casablanca: 'Political ambition can develop rapidly. For example, look at me!' Murphy, *Diplomat among Warriors* (New York, 1964), p.174.
14. Charles de Gaulle, *The Edge of the Sword* (New York, 1960), p.55.
15. Lucien Souchon, *Feue l'Armée française* (Paris, 1927).
16. Georges A. Groussard, *L'Armée et ses drames* (Paris, 1968), p.14.
17. Tournoux, *Pétain et de Gaulle*, p.78.
18. See André Beaufre, *1940, The Fall of France* (New York, 1968), pp.19-35.

19. Ibid., p.17.
20. Tournoux, *Pétain et de Gaulle*, pp.89-90.
21. De Gaulle, *The Edge of the Sword*, p.43.
22. See the November 1922 and December 1927 letters, Lucien Nachin, *Charles de Gaulle, Général de France* (Paris, 1971), pp.42, 63-4.
23. Ibid., p.54.
24. Tournoux, *Pétain et de Gaulle*, pp.102-18.
25. Charles de Gaulle, *Memoirs of Hope* (New York, 1971), p.359.
26. The passage appears in De Gaulle, *La France et son Armée*, p.91; the quotation from the exchange of letters was quoted in the *New York Times*, 6 February 1972. On the whole affair, see Pouget, *Un certain Capitaine de Gaulle*, pp.183-239, 273-83; Tournoux, *Pétain et de Gaulle*, pp.169-80; and Jacques Isorni, *Philippe Pétain* (Paris, 1972), I, pp.237-67.
27. De Gaulle, *Edge of the Sword*, p.63.
28. Charles de Gaulle, *Trois études* (Paris, 1970).
29. Statement to Yvon Bourges, quoted in J.-R. Tournoux, *Le Tourment et la fatalité* (Paris, 1974), pp.184-5.
30. Charles de Gaulle, *La Discorde chez l'ennemi* (Paris, Livre de Poche, [1973]), p.144.
31. De Gaulle, *War Memoirs*, I, pp.67-8; but cf. Maxime Weygand, *Mémoires*, 3 vols. (Paris 1950-57), I, pp.190-91 and *En lisant les Mémoires du Général de Gaulle* (Paris, 1955), pp.50-51.
32. See Louis Guitard, *Lettre sans malice à François Mauriac sur la mort du Général Weygand et quelques autres sujets* (Paris, 1966), pp.137-213, and Jacques Weygand, *Weygand, mon père* (Paris, 1970), p.467.
33. A critical estimate is in Guy Chapman, *Why France Collapsed* (London, 1968), pp.176-8, 231-7.
34. Léon Noël, *Comprendre de Gaulle* (Paris, 1972), pp.128-9.
35. Jean d'Escrienne, *Le Général m'a dit . . . 1966-1970* (Paris, 1973), pp.96-8.
36. See Noël, *Comprendre de Gaulle*, pp.103-6; d'Escrienne, *Le Général*, p.92. Georges Duhamel asked de Gaulle while the Marshal was still prisoner of the Germans in Germany, what he intended to do about Pétain. 'What can I do?' he replied. 'I'll provide him with a residence somewhere in the south, where he'll wait till Death comes to fetch him.' 7 September 1944, Claude Mauriac, *The Other de Gaulle: Diaries 1944-1954* (London, 1973), p.25.
37. Speech at Douaumont, 29 May 1966, Charles de Gaulle, *Discours et messages*, 5 vols. (Paris, 1970), V, p.37.
38. 7 September 1944, Claude Mauriac, *The Other de Gaulle*, p.25; Tournoux, *Pétain et de Gaulle*, pp.133-4.
39. Jean Mauriac, *Mort du Général*, p.127.
40. René Chambe, *Le Maréchal Juin, 'Duc du Garigliano'* (Paris, 1968), pp.430-1, 436-8; Pierre Galante, *The General!* (New York, 1968), p.228.
41. Letter of 15 June 1962, quoted in Yves Frédéric Jaffre, *Les Tribuneaux d'exception 1940-1962* (Paris, 1962), p.330. See J.-R. Tournoux, *La Tragédie du Général de Gaulle* (Paris,

1967), pp.413-18, and *Le Tourment et la fatalité*, pp.115-17.

42. 'It was General de Gaulle's misfortune to have a weakness for you,'
Jules Roy wrote in an open denunciation of Massu's confessions of
past conduct in *La vrai bataille d'Alger* (Paris, 1972), 'and which you
boasted of, to the bewilderment of many.' *J'Accuse le Général
Massu* (Paris, 1972), p.91. On the still mysterious flight to Baden-
Baden and de Gaulle's then state of mind, see J.-R. Tournoux,
Le Mois de mai du Général de Gaulle (Paris, 1969), pp.292-301,
and Philippe Alexandre, *L'Elysée en péril 2-30 mai 1968* (Paris,
1969), pp.271-92.

43. Nachin, *Charles de Gaulle*, p.64.

44. Diary, 13 March 1960, Harold Macmillan, *Memoirs*, 6 vols.
(London, 1966-   ), V, p.182.

45. Galante, *The General!*, p.203.

46. Quoted in Jaffré, *Les Tribuneaux*, p.314.

47. André Malraux, *Anti-Memoirs* (New York, 1968), pp.103-4.

48. 5 July 1940, Edmund Ironside Diary (unpublished). I remain
immensely grateful to the late Field Marshal Lord Ironside for his
generosity in giving me full access to this remarkable journal some
twenty years ago.

49. Jules Moch, *Rencontres avec de Gaulle* (Paris, 1971), p.32.

50. Charles de Gaulle, *War Memoirs, Documents*, 3 vols. (London,
1955-61), II, pp.67-8, also in United States, State Department,
Foreign Relations of the United States, Diplomatic Papers 1942,
vol.2, *Europe* (Washington, 1962), pp.541-4.

51. Charles de Gaulle, *Vers l'Armée de métier* (Paris, Livre de Poche,
1973), p.158. Cf. the telegram to his representative in Washington,
Adrien Tixier, 3 June 1942: 'We do not pretend to be the political
representatives of the French people; but we do pretend to represent
their permanent interests. We intend also to rally them to the Allied
cause in the war.' De Gaulle, *War Memoirs, Documents*, II, p.13.

52. Talks with John G. Winant, 21 May and 30 June 1942, ibid.,
pp.10, 16.

53. Colonel de Chevigné's account, in Galante, *The General!*, p.134.

54. Talk with Harold Nicolson, 2 November 1942, Nicolson, *Diaries and
Letters*, 3 vols. (London, 1966-8), II, p.256.

55. Speaking to François Goguel, quoted in Jean Mauriac, *Mort du
Général*, p.119.

56. Telegram, 1 January 1943, United States, State Department,
Foreign Relations of the United States, Diplomatic Papers 1943,
vol. 2, *Europe* (Washington, 1964), p.24.

57. Roger Trinquier, *Le Coup d'état du 13 Mai* (Paris, 1968), p.120.
'Among de Gaulle's faults,' his *directeur du cabinet*, Oliver Guichard,
would say, 'is that he thinks he can regulate military affairs by
handing out promotions and decorations. He is simply unaware of the
fact that he, de Gaulle, never made the slightest imprint on the
French army.' Diary, 1 March 1972, C.L. Sulzberger, *The Last of
the Giants* (New York, 1970), p.853.

58. Diary, 25 May 1946, Claude Mauriac, *The Other de Gaulle*, p.183.

59. Letter to Lucien Nachin, December 1927, Nachin, *Charles de Gaulle*,
p.63.

60. Quoted in Jacques de Launay, *De Gaulle and French History* (New York, 1968), p.53.

61. Nachin, *Charles de Gaulle*, p.65.

62. De Gaulle, *Vers l'Armée de métier*, p.158.

63. De Gaulle, *La France et son armée*, p.277; *Mémoirs de guerre*, 3 vols. (Paris, 1954-9), III, p.290, sentences which just do not translate effectively.

64. Diary, 15 December 1959, Sulzberger, *The Last of the Giants*, p.62.

65. Francis Bacon, 'Of Ambition,' *Essays* (London, Everyman, 1906), p.113.

66. Diary, 3 October 1946, Claude Mauriac, *The Other de Gaulle*, p.219.

67. November 1841, *Mémoires d'outre-tombe*, I, p.602.

68. Alexis de Tocqueville, *The Recollections of. . .* (New York, Meridian, 1959), p.69.

69. *The Edge of the Sword*, pp.126-7.

70. De Gaulle, *War Memoirs*, I, p.86. Note that it was this watery image which came to mind when he discussed the failure of Paul Reynaud: 'He was like a man', de Gaulle told A.J. Liebling in 1941, 'who knows he must swim a river, and who sees the other bank clear. But he was not strong enough to reach it.' A.J. Liebling, *The Road Back to Paris* (Garden City, New York, 1944), p.97.

71. Diary, 17 January 1952, Claude Mauriac, *The Other de Gaulle*, p.328. Gide's account of their talk is less dismissive: 'I asked him how and when, in his opinion, an officer should take it upon himself to disregard a command. He replied most appropriately that this could only be at a time of great events and when the feeling of duty entered into opposition with a command received.' 26 June 1943, *The Journals of André Gide*, translated by Justin O'Brien, 4 vols. (New York, 1947-51), IV.

72. See J.-L. Loubet del Bayle, *Les Non-conformistes des années 30: une tentative de renouvellement de la pensée politique française* (Paris, 1969).

73. Roger Cambon appears barely disguised, presumably because he shunned all attribution and public controversy, as 'Torcy' in Robert Mengin, *No Laurels for de Gaulle* (London, 1966), p.219.

74. Speech to the National Defence Public Interest Committee [evidently March or April 1942], de Gaulle, *War Memoirs, Documents*, I, p.279.

75. Pierre Mendès-France to de Gaulle, 8 January 1945, ibid., III, pp.153-63.

76. Quoted in Jean Mauriac, *Mort du Général*, p.76.

77. 19 September 1942, *The Diaries of Sir Alexander Cadogan*, p.478.

78. See, for instance, Edward A. Kolodziej, *French International Policy under de Gaulle and Pompidou: The Politics of Grandeur* (Ithaca, New York, 1974), p.11 and *passim*; but cf. Guy de Carmoy, *The Foreign Policies of France 1944-1968* (Chicago, 1970) which is less sanguine.

79. Quoted in Galante, *The General!*, p.193.
80. Dwight David Eisenhower, *The White House Years*, 2 vols. (New York, 1964-5), II, p.556.
81. John C. Cairns, 'De Gaulle Confronts the British: The Legacy of 1940', *International Journal*, XXIII (Spring 1968), pp.187-210.
82. Telegram, de Gaulle to General Beynet, 4 June 1945; de Gaulle, *War Memoirs, Documents*, III, p.263; Press conference, 2 June 1945, ibid., p.261.
83. De Gaulle, *War Memoirs*, III.
84. Diary, 20 March, 31 July 1946, Claude Mauriac, *The Other de Gaulle*, pp.165, 203.
85. Interview with Emanuel d'Astier de la Vigerie, *Portraits* (Paris, 1969), p.191.
86. Quoted in Tournoux, *La Tragédie du Général*, p.321.
87. Diary, 22 October 1959, Macmillan, *Memoirs*, V, p.93; de Gaulle, quoted in de Launay, *De Gaulle and the History of France*, p.159.
88. E.g., in a television interview with Michel Droit, 13 December 1965, quoted in ibid., p.224. 'The accusation of indifference to such matters so obstinately levelled against de Gaulle always struck me as absurd,' *Memoirs of Hope*, p.132.
89. André Malraux, *Les Chênes qu'on abat. . .* (Paris, 1971), pp.28, 30; see also Philippe Alexandre, *The Duel: de Gaulle and Pompidou* (New York, 1972), pp.263-5.
90. *The Prince* (London, Everyman, 1908), p.203.
91. Diary, 28 April 1946, Claude Mauriac, *The Other de Gaulle*, p.176; conversation with Jean-Marcel Jeanneney, quoted in Jean Mauriac, *Mort du Général*, p.125.
92. Machiavelli, *The Prince*, pp.79-80.
93. Conversation with Goguel, in Jean Mauriac, *Mort du Général*, p.120.
94. Malraux, *Les Chênes qu'on abat*, pp.22-3.
95. Talk with David Schoenbrun in 1959, *The Three Lives of Charles de Gaulle* (New York, 1966), p.98.
96. *The Prince*, p.78.
97. Quoted in Jean Mauriac, *Mort du Général*, p.59.
98. Sir Edward Spears, *Two Men Who Saved France: Pétain and de Gaulle* (London, 1966), p.132. An early product of this effort was 'James Marlow', *De Gaulle's France and the Key to the Coming Invasion of Germany* (London, 1940), a ninety-five page pamphlet, also published in New York *(De Gaulle and the Coming Invasion of Germany*, 1940). About 1942 or 1943 Harold Macmillan would tell Robet Murphy that the British investment in the General had then reached £70 million, Robert Murphy, *Diplomat among Warriors* (New York, 1964), p.170.
99. See Cairns, 'De Gaulle Confronts the British,' loc.cit., p.209.
100. War Cabinet Meeting, 12 Noon, 24 June 1940, Public Record Office, London, Cabinet Papers, WM 178 (40), p.371.
101. Hugh Dalton Diary, 26, 28 June 1940, Library of the London School of Economics. See P.M.H. Bell, *A Certain Eventuality: Britain and the Fall of France* (London, 1974), p.191 ff.

102. Quoted by David Dilks in *The Diaries of Sir Alexander Cadogan*, p.302.
103. Cadogan thought, 'Catroux is double-crossing de G. De G. evidently thinks so too!' (3 April 1943, *The Diaries of Sir Alexander Cadogan*, p.518.) There was no evidence for this, though the perhaps anxious tone of de Gaulle's telegrams to Catroux (which undoubtedly were intercepted and read in London) may have occasioned the suspicion. E.g., that of 31 March 1943, de Gaulle, *War Memoirs, Documents*, II, pp.149-50. See Georges Catroux, *Dans la Bataille de Méditerranée* (Paris, 1949).
104. Quoted in de Launay, *De Gaulle and the History of France*, p.53. 'He said,' Duff Cooper noted in his diary after dining with the General in January 1944, 'that he tries, every day, for a short time to imagine himself looking down on events without prejudice and from the point of view of the future historian.' *Old Men Forget, The Autobiography of Duff Cooper (Viscount Norwich)* (London, 1953), p.320.
105. 20 January 1941, Nicolson, *Diaries and Letters*, II, p.138.
106. 20 October 1942, *Chips, The Diaries of Sir Henry Channon*, Robert Rhodes James (ed.) (London, 1967), pp.339-40.
107. André Labarthe, quoted 31 April 1942 in Nicolson, *Diaries and Letters*, II, pp.224-5.
108. 18 January 1942, de Gaulle, *War Memoirs, Documents*, I, p.425.
109. Quoted in de Launay, *De Gaulle and the History of France*, p.45. See Bell, *A Certain Eventuality*, pp.199-212.
110. Duncan Grinnell Milne, *The Triumph of Integrity: A Portrait of Charles de Gaulle* (New York, 1962), p.162.
111. Statement to Schoenbrun, *The Three Lives of Charles de Gaulle*, p.125. Cf. the far less clear statement of the 'perpetual bondage' he thereafter assumed, *War Memoirs*, I, p.136. According to Colonel de Larminat who met him at Brazzaville, de Gaulle said, 'Well then, shall we go on?' (Edgard de Larminat, *Chroniques irréverencieuses* (Paris, 1962), p.171). But his mind would seem to have been by then perfectly made up.
112. 20 August 1946, *The Other de Gaulle*, p.303.
113. Minute, 27 May 1942, quoted by Woodward, *British Foreign Policy*, II, p.333.
114. Diary, 22 January 1943, Lord Moran, *Churchill: Taken from the Diaries of Lord Moran: The Struggle for Survival 1940-1965* (Boston, 1966), p.88. There is no doubt of Churchill's considerable hostility, as there is none of the General's relentless opposition to every action or gesture, great or small, which he interpreted as even the most minute infraction of French sovereignty. 'You like the man,' the Prime Minister would throw at Duff Cooper when he tried to explain de Gaulle's point of view, 'I don't.' Cooper, *Old Men Forget*, p.315.
115. De Gaulle to the Free French Delegation, 13 August 1941, *War Memoirs, Documents*, I, p.214.
116. On the Marshall incident, see Forrest C. Pogue, *George C. Marshall*,

3 vols. (New York, 1963-73), III, pp.401-2.
117. Dulles quoting Eisenhower to David Schoenbrun, February 1959, quoted in Townshend Hoopes, *The Devil and John Foster Dulles* (Boston, 1973), p.474.
118. 23 April 1961, Charles de Gaulle, *Discours et messages*, 5 vols. (Paris, 1970), III, pp.306-8; *Major Addresses, Statements and Press Conferences of General Charles de Gaulle 19 May 1958 — 31 January 1964* (New York, French Embassy Press and Information Division, n.d.), pp.127-8.
119. *The Prince*, pp.141-3.
120. Press conference, 21 April 1944, de Gaulle, *War Memoirs, Documents*, II, p.329, and see de Gaulle to Giraud, 8 April 1944, ibid., pp.263-4.
121. Henry Taylor, *The Statesman: An Ironical Treatise on the Art of Succeeding* [1836] (Cambridge, 1927), p.76.
122. Minute to Eden, 13 June 1944, quoted in Woodward, *British Foreign Policy*, III, p.62.
123. Diary, 29 November 1961, Macmillan, *Memoirs*, V, p.428.
124. Press conference, 14 January 1963, De Gaulle, *Discours et messages*, IV, p.62; *Major Addresses*, p.213.
125. *The Prince*, p.63.
126. Ibid., p.182.
127. Janine Mossuz, *André Malraux et le gaullisme* (Paris, 1970), pp.67-8.
128. A lively and unsympathetic dissection of de Gaulle's words and character, is Jean-François Revel, *Le Style du Général* (Paris, 1959).
129. De Gaulle, *Memoirs of Hope*, p.315.
130. General Dulac was categoric that when he reported at Colombey on the Algiers situation, 28 May, de Gaulle said that while he could not then take sides as between Paris and Algiers — since he must seem to be called in as arbiter by the whole nation — Dulac should tell Salan to do what was necessary (i.e., to threaten destruction of the Pflimlin Government by force, or at least a show of force). André Dulac, *Nos guerres perdues: Levant 1941. Indochine 1951-53. Algérie 1958-1960* (Paris, 1969), pp.88-9. See also Jacques Soustelle, *L'Espérance trahie* (Paris, 1962), pp.45-6 and *Vingt-huit ans de gaullisme* (Paris, 1968), pp.145-7.
131. To Pierre Bertaux, quoted in Robert Aron, *The Liberation of France August 1944 — May 1945*, 2 vols. (London, 1963-4), II, p.238.
132. 'Of Empire,' *Essays*, p.61.
133. *The Prince*, p.177.
134. Quoted in de Launay, *De Gaulle and the History of France*, pp.35-6.
135. Telegram, de Gaulle to Médecin général Sicé, 2 April 1942, for Leclerc, de Gaulle, *War Memoirs, Documents*, I, p.416.
136. Diary, 22 January 1943, Moran, *Churchill*, p.88.
137. De Gaulle, *War Memoirs, Documents*, I, pp.46-8.
138. Diary, 19 May 1962, Macmillan, *Memoirs*, VI, p.118.

139. Statement to David Schoenbrun, *The Three Lives of Charles de Gaulle*, p.98. Well-intentioned but naïve, Field Marshal Smuts had once tried — before the battering blows of 1943-44 — to assure de Gaulle that Great Britain had no *arrière pensée* concerning French interests in the Middle East or elsewhere, pleading with him to resolve the matter directly in London since 'I am confident that a personal talk between two big men like you will dissipate the atmosphere of misunderstanding' (Smuts to de Gaulle, 16 September 1942, in W.K. Hancock and Jean van der Poel (eds.), *Selections from the Smuts Papers*, 7 vols. (Cambridge, 1966-73), VI, No. 580). But no one could help either protagonist, though many tried: 'Clemmie said she had given Winston a Caudle curtain lecture this morning on the importance of not quarrelling with de Gaulle.' Diary, 10 January 1944, Cooper, *Old Men Forget*, p.318.

140. David C. Gordon, *The Passing of French Algeria* (London, 1966), pp.53-4; Yves Courrière, *La Guerre d'Algérie*, 4 vols. (Paris, 1968-71), I, pp.39-46; Claude Paillat, *Vingt ans qui déchirèrent la France*, 2 vols. (Paris, 1969-72), I, pp.22-57.

141. Quoted in Galante, *The General!*, p.17. Yet it should be said, too, that the extravagance of the Gaullist vocabulary may mislead us. He delighted in using coarse expressions and dealt regularly in hyperbole. See Tournoux, *Le Tourment et la fatalité*, p.397.

142. Noël, *Comprendre de Gaulle*, pp.100-1.

143. Tournoux, *La Tragédie du Général*, pp.442-54.

144. Ibid., pp.413-18; Tournoux, *Le Tourment et la fatalité*, pp.109-11; Alexandre, *The Duel*, pp.86-92.

145. Quoted in Malraux, *Les Chênes*, p.108.

146. Diary, July 1944, in *The Mackenzie King Record*, J.W. Pickersgill and D.F. Forster (eds.), 4 vols. (Toronto, 1960-70), II, p.49; also John S.D. Eisenhower, *Strictly Personal* (New York, 1974), p.279.

147. Diary, 13 March 1960, Macmillan, *Memoirs*, V, p.183.

148. Oliver Lyttelton, Viscount Chandos, *The Memoirs of Lord Chandos* (London, 1962), p.249.

149. Quoted in de Launay, *De Gaulle and the History of France*, p.117.

150. Conversation with Sulzberger, 22 December 1961, *The Last of the Giants*, p.831; Soustelle, *L'Espérance trahie*, p.94.

151. Quoted in Tournoux, *La Tragédie du Général*, p.432.

152. Telegram, Jefferson Caffery to Secretary of State, Paris, 28 January 1945, 11 p.m., United States, Department of State, *Foreign Relations of the United States, Diplomatic Papers*, vol. 4, *Europe* (Washington, 1968), p.666.

153. Taylor, *The Statesman*, p.177.

154. See the remarkable essay by Stanley and Inge Hoffmann, 'De Gaulle as Political Artist: The Will to Grandeur,' in Stanley Hoffmann, *Decline or Renewal? France since the 1930s* (New York, 1974), pp.202-53.

155. Spaak, *Combats inachevés*, II, p.167.

156. Churchill telephoning to Charles Peake, quoted in Diary, 12 March,

1943, Nicolson, *Diaries and Letters*, II, p.284. For his part, de Gaulle
seems to have referred to the Prime Minister as 'le monstre de
Downing Street' (Galante, *The General!*, p.32), but he himself got
much the worst of the verbal battle. Among the *bons mots* and
cracks making the wartime rounds was Admiral Dickens' remark on
being summoned to de Gaulle during the Admiral Muselier affair:
'The General will only make a face like a female llama surprised
bathing' (16 March 1942, *The Diaries of Sir Alexander Cadogan*,
p.441). Years later, this one was still around and being attributed
to Churchill. Diary, 6 December 1959, Moran, *Churchill*, p.813.

157. Tournoux, *La Tragédie du Général*, p.13.
158. De Gaulle, *Memoirs of Hope*, pp.300-1.
159. Harold Wilson, *The Labour Government 1964-1970: A Personal
Record* (London, 1971), p.406.
160. Quoted in d'Escrienne, *Le Général m'a dit*, p.20.
161. Quoted in Jean Mauriac, *Mort du Général*, p.140.
162. In addition to Jean Mauriac, see Jacques Chapus, *Mourir à
Colombey* (Paris, 1971).
163. Jean Mauriac, *Mort du Général*, pp.22, 28.
164. Conversation with Malraux, *Les Chênes*, p.79.
165. D'Escrienne, *Le Général m'a dit*, pp.72, 256.
166. Adams to Henry Cabot Lodge, 6 October 1879, *Letters of Henry
Adams 1858-1918*, Worthington Chauncey Ford (ed.), 2 vols.
(Boston, 1930-38), I, p.314.

Contributors

Stephen E. Amrbose, a native of Wisconsin, is Professor of History at the University of New Orleans. He has taught at the Naval War College (where he was E.J. King Professor) and Kansas State University (as D.D. Eisenhower Professor of War and Peace). The author of twelve books of political and military history, including *Rise to Globalism* (Pelican, 1971) and *Duty, Honor, Country: A History of West Point* (John Hopkins, 1966), Ambrose's work at the Johns Hopkins University with President's Eisenhower's official papers gave him access to material (as well as to the man himself) that led to his book *The Supreme Commander: The War Years of General Dwight D. Eisenhower* (Doubleday, 1970). In addition, Ambrose's articles have appeared regularly in such publications as *American Heritage*, *The Progressive*, and *The New York Review of Books*. His latest work, *Crazy Horse and Custer: The Parallel Lives of Two American Warriors*, is a dual biography.

John C. Cairns, Professor of History at the University of Toronto, is the author of a book on contemporary France and articles on various aspects of French, British and international affairs in the twentieth century.

Peter Dennis was born in Adelaide and educated at the University of Adelaide and Duke University. Since 1969 he has taught at The Royal Military College of Canada, Kingston, Ontario. He is the author of *Decision by Default: Peacetime Conscription and British Defence, 1919-1939* (Routledge and Duke University Press, 1972).

Roger Graham was born in Montreal and educated at United College, Winnipeg, and the University of Toronto. From 1947 to 1968 he was a member of the Department of History at the University of Saskatchewan. Since 1968 he has been Douglas Professor of Canadian History at Queen's University,

Kingston. He is the author of *Arthur Meighen, a Biography* (3 volumes, University of Toronto Press, 1963).

Martin Kitchen is Associate Professor of History at Simon Fraser University, British Columbia. He is the author of *The German Officer Corps 1890-1914* (Clarendon, 1968); *A Military History of Germany* (Weidenfeld and Nicolson, 1975); and *Fascism* (Macmillan, 1976).

Adrian Preston has been Associate Professor of History at RMC, Kingston since 1965. In 1971-72 he held the Chair of Military and Strategic Studies at Acadia University, Nova Scotia. He has published *In Relief of Gordon* (India, 1967), *The South Africa Diaries of Sir Garnet Wolseley, 1875* (Cape Town, 1971), *The South African Journals of Sir Garnet Wolseley, 1879-80*, (Cape Town, 1973) and is the co-editor, with Peter Dennis, of *Covenants and Swords: Essays in Honour of the Centenary of the Royal Military College of Canada, 1876-1976*, (London, 1976). He has lectured at the Indian and Canadian Defence and Staff Colleges and has published many articles in military and learned journals in Great Britain, Canada, USA, India and South Africa. Adrian Preston is a Canadian Commissioner on the International Commission for the Study of Miliary History.

Hugh Thomas is Professor of History at the University of Reading and Chairman of that University's School of Contemporary European Studies. He is known for his works on the *Spanish Civil War* (London, 1961), *Cuba* (1971) and *The Suez Affair* (1967). He is at the moment writing a study of the idea of progress.

Index

Abercrombie, Sir Ralph, 25
Adams, Henry, 166
Adenauer, Konrad, 153
Alanbrooke, F.M. Viscount, 49, 50, 114, 117
Alfonso XIII, King, 85, 86, 91
Algeria, 143, 144, 158, 161, 162
Alison, 22
Allenby, F.-M. Viscount, 20, 26, 37; Wavell on, 41, 45, 46, 49
al Misri, Gen. Aziz Ali, 45
America; military history and tradition, 14, 16, 17, 37-8; strategic responsibilities, 16; War of Independence, 23, 24
Amery, L.S., 47
Anglo American Combined Chiefs of Staff, 11, 15
Anido, Martinez, 81, 82
Annet, Armand, 151
Astry, Col. Millán, 84
Ataturk, Kemal, 45
Attlee, C.R. (Earl), 46
Auxiliary Labour Law (*Hilfsdienstgesetz*), 62, 63
Azana, Manuel, 85

Bacon, Francis, 147, 161
Baker, Josephine, 163
Baldwin, Stanley (Earl), 40
Barea, Sergeant, 85
Baring, Capt. Evelyn (Lord Cromer), 20
Bastien-Thiry, Col., 162, 163
Bauer, Colonel, 58, 64, 65, 68
Beaufre, André, 138
Bennett, R.B., 109
Bentham, Jeremy, 27
Berlin, and Second World War, 118, 119, 120, 126, 127, 130
Bernhardi, 28

Bethmann Hollweg, Theobald von, 59, 61, 65, 66
Beynet, Gen., 152
Bidault, Georges, 164
Bismarck, Otto von, 65, 67
Blomberg, 75
Blanco, Admiral Carrero, 90
Boulanger, Gen. George, 28
Bradley, Gen. Omar, 115, 117, 119
Brecht, Bertolt, 77
Brest-Litovsk, Treaty of, 67
Brezhnev, Leonid, 153
Bridges, Styles, 113
Brinkmanship, 123, 124, 125
Brüning, Heinrich, 71, 72
Buchan, John, 93, 94, 99, 105, 110
Buller, Sir Redvers, 32
Burgfrieden, 60
Butler, 20
Byng, Viscount, 84, 93-110; relations with Mackenzie King, 93, 96-110; unconventionality, 95
Byng, Lady, 93, 99, 100, 101, 102, 107, 108, 109

Cabanellas, 86
Cadogan, Sir Alexander, 155
Caesarism, 9, 18, 31
Cambon, Roger, 149, 150
Cambridge, Duke of, 30
Canaris, Admiral, 86
Cardwell, Edward (Viscount), 30
Carlyle, Thomas, 26, 80
Carnarvon, Lord, 33
Catroux, Gen. Georges, 156
Central Intelligence Agency (CIA), 12, 129, 131
Chamberlain, Joseph, 33

Chamberlain, Neville, 40, 155
Chanak crisis, 96
Channon, Sir Henry, 156
Charleston, battle of, 24
Chateaubriand, vicomte de, 135, 147, 148
Chelmsford, 30
Chiang Kai-shek, 113, 130
Childers, Hugh, 33
Churchill, Lord Randolph, 33
Churchill, Sir Winston S., and De Gaulle, 39, 136, 150, 155, 157, 158, 159, 162, 163, 164; and India, 38, 46, 47, 48; military outlook, 15, 26, 36, 44; and USSR, 117, 118, 119; and Wavell, 38, 43, 46, 47, 48
Clark, Gen. Mark, 124
Clausewitz, Karl von, 10, 27, 28
Clay, Gen. Lucius D., 18, 38
Cold War, 113, 129, 130, 131, 132
Commander-in-Chief, office of, 21, 22, 23, 24, 34
Continental Army, 10, 24
Coty, René, 161
Cromwell, Oliver, 10, 19, 21, 23, 39, 41; Cromwellianism, 22, 35
Cruttwell, C.R.M.F., 48
Cunliffe, Marcus, 42
Curragh incident, 32, 36, 43

Daladier, Edouard, 140, 141
Dalton, Hugh (Lord), 155
Daniel, Jean, 144
Debré, Michel, 161, 165
De Gaulle, Charles, 17, 19, 126, 135-66; and Algeria, 161, 162; Churchill on, 136, 157, 158, 159, 162; and Free France, 150, 151, 156, 161; military outlook, 42, 44, 46, 137-48; oratory, 50; personality, 163; publications, 139, 140, 141, 144, 146, 147, 148; and Roosevelt, 39, 144, 145, 150, 156; statesmanship, 39, 40, 41, 45-6, 149, 164
Degaulle, Philippe, 165

Delbruck, 69
Dien Bien Phu, 125, 126
Dietrich, 71
Dilke, Sir Charles, 33
Disraeli, Benjamin, 20, 31
Dulles, J.F., 120, 123, 124, 125, 158
Dundas, Henry, 21

Ebert, Friedrich, 67, 68, 69, 70
Eden, Sir Anthony (Lord Avon), 158
Ehrhard, Ludwig, 153
Eisenhower, Dwight D., 113-32, 17, 18, 19, 38, 41, 44, 113-32, 165; and Berlin, 118, 119, 127; defence policy, 114, 121, 122; and De Gaulle, 151, 152, 158, 162; hatred of Communism, 113, 120, 121; New Look policy, 121, 122, 123; and Korean War, 124-5; military outlook, 42, 43; and USSR, 128, 129-32

Fabeck, Col. von, 56
Falkenhayn, 56, 57, 58, 60, 61, 62, 75
Fascism, Spanish, 87, 88, 89
Fraga, Manuel, 92
France, military politics in, 28-9
Franco, Francisco, 39, 40, 43, 79-92; and Civil War, 85-7; Fascism of, 87, 88, 89; military outlook, 41, 42, 79; and Morocco, 84-5; political beliefs, 92; power methods, 88-92
Fraser, Lady Antonia, 14

Gaither Report, 128, 129
Geneva summit meeting, 130, 131, 132
George V, King, 95
German Army: and Hitler, 14; military attitudes, 11, 28
Gide, André, 148
Giraud, Gen. Henri, 156, 159
Gladstone, W.E., 32, 33
Goebbels, Josef, 71, 74

Goltz, 28
Gordon, Gen. C.G., 33, 35
Gough, Gen. Sir Hubert, 32
Grant, Gen. U.S., 18, 19
Groener, Gen., 62, 63, 64, 71
Grousset, Pascal, 138
Grzesinski, 71
Guibert, 46
Guy, Claude, 146

Haig, F.-M. Sir Douglas (Earl),
    26, 35, 37, 49, 50
Halibut Treaty, 96
Hamburg Points, 68
Hamilton, Gen. Sir Ian, 35
Hamley, Gen., 33
Hammerstein, 73
Hartington, 32
Hedilla, Manuel, 88
Herriot, Edouard, 156
Hindenburg, Paul von, 55-77,
    165; and Ebert regime, 67-9;
    and Hitler, 72, 73, 74, 75;
    military qualities, 56, 75-6;
    Presidency, 70-5, 76, 77; war
    appointments and aims,
    55-67; and Weimar Republic,
    69, 70, 71, 72
Hitler, Adolf, 89; German Army
    and, 14; and Hindenburg,
    71-2, 73, 74, 75; *putsch*, 69
Hoare, Sir Samuel, 87
Ho Chi Minh, 125
Hodges, Gen, Courtney, 115, 116
Hoffman, Stanley, 40
Hoffman, 56
Holtzendorff, 66
Howard, Michael, 12, 20, 26, 36
Howicke Commission, 23
Hugenberg, Alfred, 71, 72
Hughes, Emmet John, 124
Hughes, Col. Sam, 44
Humphrey, Hubert H., 130
Huntington, S.P., 13, 16

Ignatieff, Gen., 20
Imperial Defence College, 11, 37
India: Army, 15, 16, 34, 47;
    Britain and, 29; independence,
    15, 38, 46

Industrial War College, 11
Ironside, F.-M. Lord, 144

Jackson, Andrew, 19
James, Henry, 30
Janowitz, M., 16
Johnson, Lyndon B., 130, 151
Jomini, 27
Jouhaud, Gen. Edmond, 163
Juan Carlos, Prince (later King),
    91
Juin, Marshal Alphonse, 138, 143

Kapp *putsch*, 68, 69
Kempton, Murray, 114
Kennedy, Jacqueline, 163
Kennedy, John F., 127, 130
Khartoum, 33, 35
Khrushchev, Nikita, 126, 127,
    129, 130, 131, 132, 151
King, W.L. Mackenzie, relations
    with Viscount and Lady
    Byng, 93-110
Kitchener, F.-M. Earl, 31, 33,
    34, 35, 36, 44, 48, 49, 57
Knowland, William, 113
Korean War, 113, 121, 124, 125
Kriegsamt (War Office), 62, 63
Krupp, 69
Kuhlmann, 66

La Discorde chez l'ennemi, 141
La France et son Armée, 140,
    147
Lang, Kurt, 137
Larminat, Gen. Edgard de, 143
Lattre de Tassigny, Gen. de, 152
Laurier, Sir Wilfrid, 97, 104
Lausanne, Treaty of, 96
Lebanon, 127, 129, 152
Leclerc, Gen. 157, 161
Le Fil de l'épée, 139, 146, 148
Lequis, Gen., 68
Liddell Hart, B.H., 14
Lincoln, Gen. Benjamin, 24
Lisagor, Peter, 127
Llano, Gen. Queipo de, 86
Lloyd George, David (Earl), 37
Longford, Lady, 14
Louvois, Marquis de, 146

Ludendorff, Erich, 58, 63; and
Hindenburg, 55, 56; and
Hitler, 69, 76; and military
domination, 14, 66, 141
Lushington, 49
Luther, 71
Lyttelton, Oliver (Viscount
Chandos), 163

MacArthur, Gen. Douglas, 18,
20, 25, 32, 38
McCarthy, Joseph R., 113
Macdonald, Sir John, 104
Machiavelli, Niccolo, 154, 155,
158, 160
Mackensen, F.-M. August von,
71, 75
McCoy, John, 17
MacMahon, Marshal, 19, 28
Macmillan, Harold: champion of
peace, 132; and de Gaulle,
152, 153, 159, 162, 163
MacNaughton, Gen. A.G.L., 12
Malraux, André, 144, 149, 152,
153, 160
Mao Tse-tung, 19, 130
Marchand, Gen. Jean B., 32
Marlborough, John Churchill,
Duke of, 22, 45
Marquez, Gabriel García, 83
Marshall, Gen. George C., 18, 20,
41, 117, 158
Marx, 69, 70, 72
Massu, Gen. Jacques, 143
Master-General of Ordnance,
title of, 23, 34
Mauriac, Claude, 147, 157
Maurice, Gen., 25
Mayer, Emile, 139
Meighen, Arthur, 98, 100;
budget policy, 103; defeat,
110; and Mackenzie King,
109; and Lord Byng, 95, 99,
105, 107, 108
Meissner, 74
Mémoires de guerre, 147
Mendès-France, Pierre, 150
Michelet, Jules, 154
Military clubs, 23
Military Institutions and Policies

of the British Empire, 23
Mitterand, François, 161
Moch, Jules, 144
Mola, Gen., 86
Moltke, Gen. Ludwig von, 57
Monnet, Jean, 147
Montgomery, F.-M. Viscount,
18; and Eisenhower, 114, 115,
116, 117, 118; professionalism,
26, 38
Moore, Gen. Sir John, 26
Moran, Lord, 163
Morocco War, 81, 83, 84-5
Morton, Desmond, 155
Muller, 74
Mulock, Sir William, 97
Mussolini, Benito, 88

Nachin, Lucien, 138, 143, 146
Napier, Sir William, 22
Napoleon I, 19, 41, 42, 136
Nasser, Gamal Abdel, 45
Navarro, Arias, 90, 92
Nazi Party, 73
New Model Army, 10
Nicolson, Sir Harold, 156
Nixon, Richard M., 113, 125
Noël, Léon, 142
North Atlantic Treaty
Organisation (NATO), 123
Nuclear weapons, 122, 123, 128,
129

Opus Dei order, 88, 90

Palewski, Gaston, 145
Papen, Franz von, 72, 73, 74, 75
Pasley, Sir Charles, 21, 23
Patton, Gen. George, 115, 116,
118, 119
Peake, Charles, 164
Perón, Juan, 89
Pershing, Gen. J.J., 37
Pétain, Marshal Henri, 19, 40,
137, 138, 139, 140, 142
Pinay, Antoine, 164
Polavieja, Gen., 83
Political generals, 27-36
Pompidou, Georges, 162
Prittwitz, 55

Reynaud, Paul, 137, 140, 141, 146
Rhee, Dr Syngman, 125
Ridgway, Gen. Matthew, 125, 126
Reiber, Capt., 87
Rivera, José Antonio de, 88
Rivera, Gen. Primo de, 81, 82
Roberts, F.-M. Lord, 29, 30, 35, 49
Robertson, F.-M. Sir William, 37, 50
Rockefeller Foundation, 128
Rohm *putsch*, 74
Roosevelt, Franklin D., 18; and Berlin, 118; and de Gaulle, 39, 144, 145, 150, 156; and Three-Power alliance, 117
Roosevelt, Theodore, 19, 26, 32
RPF movement, 152, 160

Salan, Gen. Raoul, 143, 144, 163
Sanjurjo rising, 85
Schleicher, 72, 73, 74
Schlieffen, 55, 56, 58, 61
Schumann, Maurice, 151
Scott, Sir Walter, 9, 13, 48
Seeckt, 69, 70
Segura, Cardinal, 90
Sladen, Arthur, 107-8
Slim, F.-M. Viscount, 26, 50
Soldier-statesmen: British and American view of, 18, 24-5, 26; definition of, 18-20
Solis, José, 90, 92
Spaak, Paul-Henri, 136, 164
Spears, Sir Edward L., 146, 155
Spirit of the Beehive (film), 89
Sputnik, 128
Staff Colleges, 27, 28
Stahlhelm, 71
Stalin, Joseph, 87, 89
Stanley, Col. F.A., 33
Stegerwald, 71
Stephenson, 30
Stinnes, Hugo, 58
Stresemann, Gustav, 69
Submarine warfare, 61, 62
Sudreau, Pierre, 164
Syria, 152

Tannenberg, 56
Taylor, Sir Henry, 159, 164
Taylor, Gen. Maxwell, 122
Tel el Kebir, battle of, 33
Temple, Richmond, 155
Templer, F.-M. Sir Gerald, 18, 20
Tirpitz, Admiral Alfred von, 69
Tocqueville, Alexis de, 148
Trinquier, Col., 146
Truman, Harry S., 25, 120, 121, 125, 132
Twining, Gen. Nathan, 125

U-2 flights, 129, 131
United Nations, 117

Valentini, 66
Vauban, Marshal, 138, 139
Verdun, 57, 61
Verein Deutscher Eisenhuttenleute, 58
Versailles, Treaty of, 68, 70
Vers l'Armée de metier, 139, 144, 146
Vietnam, 125, 126
Vigny, Alfred de, 27, 46

Waldersee, 32, 55
Wales, Prince of (later King Edward VIII), 102
War: Department, 24; Minister of, 34; Secretaryship of, 21, 22, 24
Washington, George, 10, 18, 19, 22, 24, 39; as head of state, 42, 43, 44
Wavell, F.-M. Earl, 19, 26, 43, 45, 50; and Allenby, 41, 45, 46, 49; and Churchill, 38, 46-7, 48; military qualities, 41, 42; as Viceroy, 20, 32, 37, 38, 46, 47, 48
Weimar Republic, 60, 64, 70, 71, 72, 76
Wellington, Arthur Wellesley, Duke of, 30, 36, 39, 43, 50; Army policy, 23; despatches, 22; military qualities, 26, 41, 42; as Prime Minister, 9, 22, 23, 25, 48-9; Scott on, 9

Wells, H.G., 45
Weygand, Gen. Maxime, 141, 142, 156
Weyler, Gen., 83
Whitaker, John, 92
Whitehead, Don, 114
Wild, 66
William II, Kaiser, 55, 59, 65, 66, 68
Willis-O'Connor, Col. H., 95
Wilson, Harold, 164
Wilson, F.-M. Sir Henry (Lord), 37
Wilson, Woodrow, 32

Winant, John G., 145
Wolfe, Gen. James, 25
Wolseley, F.-M. Sir Garnet (Viscount), 49, 50; Life of Marlborough, 34; military politics, 25, 26, 29, 30-6
Wood Leonard, 32

Yalta Conference, 118
Young Plan, 71
Ypres, battles of, 56, 57

Zaragoza Military Academy, 41, 85